FIGHTING
IT OUT

with
DIFFICULT *-if not impossible*
PEOPLE

Raymond K. Tucker, Ph.D
Bowling Green State University

K H

Kendall/Hunt
Publishing Company
Dubuque, Iowa

TO MY FOUR ANGELS:

BESS, DEANNA, MYRNA, AND LESLIE

Contents

Preface

This book is written for the millions of human beings worldwide who need help in facing up to—and facing down—the difficult (if not impossible) people in their lives.

About the Author

Dr. Tucker is a New Englander by birth.

He earned his bachelor's degree from the University of Denver. His master's and doctorate were conferred by Northwestern University. Post-doctoral study, Harvard.

With a new Ph.D. in hand, he accepted a position in the training and education division of United States Steel Corporation, Gary, Indiana (now called USX). But teaching was to ultimately win out over the industrial life. He left big steel for Purdue University. He moved on to Western Illinois University; then on to Bowling Green, Ohio.

At Bowling Green State University he is a professor and serves as chair of the Department of Interpersonal and Public Communication.

Dr. Tucker has received four highly prestigious awards for his teaching. Western Illinois University honored him with the Most Outstanding Professor award. This was followed by an award for excellence in seminar presentation by the Continuing Education division at Bowling Green. Then in 1982 he became the first Bowling Green faculty member to receive the Master Teacher Award. And in 1986 he received the covetous faculty excellence award from the student government. Finally, in 1986 he was the faculty member in the College of Arts and Sciences cited most frequently by graduating seniors as contributing most significantly to their educational development.

The world of industry and organizations has responded to Dr. Tucker in a similar manner. And, as of this date, they have presented him with over 100 awards, citations and honors for his presentations, seminars, and consulting.

As an author Dr. Tucker has likewise distinguished himself. He has co-authored two books: *Essentials of Public Speaking,* and *Research in Speech Communication.* He has published over 50 articles and has presented an equal number of scholarly papers at professional conventions.

Dr. Tucker spent over twenty years researching the current volume. During this time he also presented over 2,000 seminars of various kinds on such topics as Working Smarter, Fighting Back After 40!, and Dealing with Difficult People. In 1985 Dan Rather featured Dr. Tucker and his Difficult People seminar twice on the CBS evening news.

Dr. Tucker is also in demand for keynote addresses and motivational speeches. Over 350,000 people have heard him talk. His public speaking is inimitable: tight organization, a uniquely entertaining style, and the inclusion of vital and practical information that has been obtained directly from the front lines of life.

1
On Getting to Know DPs

The typical seminar in the United States is a failure. Not because we don't tell people a lot of interesting things. We do. The real reason is that we don't tell them the things they need to know to survive and prosper.

I know. I've presented over 2000 of them, most of them having to do with some aspect of communication. Typically, I told people how wonderful life is when we all communicate well. The people who attended took good notes, nodded at the right times, and laughed at my attempts at humor. When the seminar wound down and the questions were fired at me I tensed up.

"I have this kind of person in my organization. How can I resolve the problem?" someone would say. My response was, "I don't know." Then another: "What do you do when someone refuses to listen to you?" or "This person has been treating me rotten for the past year. How can I turn her around?" My answers, again, were the same: "I don't have information on how to deal with those kinds of people." I didn't.

The seminars continued. So did the embarrassing questions. One day I was hit with: "This woman is spreading terrible rumors about me. How do I shut her up?" I told her there wasn't an awful lot I could tell her other than to try talking to the woman. That evening in my motel I reflected on the day. Yes, I was giving people the best information available on what good communication was all about. It wasn't enough. I wasn't giving them a program to deal with the people in their lives that were really driving them crazy, making them want to stay home rather than go to work, or who were just plain treating them in trashy ways! I needed to know more. About whom? About these difficult people—the nigh on to impossible people—that cause so much misery in our lives, the ones that simply never seem to let up.

It took less than three days of research to find out that virtually nothing had been done in that area. Sure there were a few ideas scattered throughout the social and behavioral science literature. But it added up to a big fat zero. Conclusion: We know nothing about difficult people— how they got that way, how they think they can get away with it, and—most importantly—how to fight back! People by the score recounted how this small minority was causing them grief all out of proportion to their numbers. The time for action, I told myself, had arrived. I made a commitment. In the next few years I would spend the bulk of my consulting time finding out what DPs were all about. I did. Fortunately the opportunities were there. I worked with over 130 organizations. I staged hundreds of seminars, sometimes over ten in a single week. I listened, I watched. I interviewed or otherwise communicated with over 110,000 people including hundreds of people who were on someone's hit list as a DP.

I'm still learning, finding out more of what goes on in the heads of those people who seem bent on making *our* lives miserable. And I'm still refining my approach. The remainder of this book outlines what I found and the strategies and tactics—all positive—I recommend.

How much faith can you put in my system? By actual count I've found there is a 90% success rate if you follow it. This means that there will be significant—noticeable—improvement, but not necessarily a total cure. The cure may take a little longer. You'll have to persist. But if you hang in there, there'll be one less DP in your life. More on what you can expect later on.

What I Found

Years of working in the DP arena leads me to conclude that:

1. Virtually all DPs know that some others see them in a negative light, or—expressed differently—are on to their game! In fact, DPs readily admit to treating some people—never everyone—very badly.
2. About 5% of those thought to be DPs haven't the slightest idea that they are perceived that way. The word is "oblivious". When they find out, they're crushed, shocked. Apparently they have received no feedback. Or the feedback that has come their way has been too subtle for them. In a very real sense, then, they can be said to be living in a dream world.
3. By directly confronting DPs, by using your head, by applying principles of communication that we've known for years—you can turn DPs around, resolve your conflict, get better treatment, these and more. There's no *special* talent required. You already have the necessary skills. You just have to generate the courage.
4. The key to dealing with DPs is *personal communicative power*. It's the heart of my system. It says this: DPs, and everyone for that matter, are affected most by those who demonstrate personal power in their communication.
5. Positiveness is the central ingredient in communicative power. It's a basic fact of life. It underlies my system, permeating every element. The message is simple: negativism is out. But, then, it never was in! It means that we concentrate on what is possible. It means that we jettison methods designated to destroy, fake, bluff, or "get" that DP.
6. Each DP is unique. Yet they have many common characteristics—similar ways of thinking and behaving. This means that one system can be effective in dealing with all of them. Further, though there are thousands of them, they are easily categorized and the categories are few.

The New Attitude

Americans have never had the reputation for taking a lot of guff from anyone. Still, until the past few years, too many of us have been content with suffering—with taking it! DPs have always been there. They're not a new force to be reckoned with. We've just too often let them off the hook, explained them away, felt there's nothing that could be done.

That day is over. I'm happy to report that the new attitude fast gaining momentum in this country is contained in the words "Fight Back! We have no intention of taking it anymore!" The fears, the excuses, are being laid to rest and the fight is on! Is "fight" the appropriate word? Yes! Life is—or should be—conceived of as a good, clean, healthy, positive fight. It implies that nothing worthwhile ever happens unless we take positive action—until we do something. It's the attitude that makes sense.

What I have to say in every page of this book is dedicated to the idea that positive fighters win, both in the short and long runs of life. That's what thousands of Americans have told me. They demonstrate it every day. I believe they are right.

R. K. Tucker's Writing Style

Self-help books abound with illustrations. "Joe is an office manager and Jill is his secretary. For several months Jill has felt that Joe has been rude and insensitive in his behavior, especially in the presence of others. . . ."

Another: "Joan Adair (not her real name) came to me for therapy. Joan was on the verge of divorcing her husband of three years, (Ned)—not his real name, either. . . ."

For many texts there are fifty words of advice to every thousand words of illustration. I have nothing against illustrations. Some people love them. Others find them boring and unnecessary. To my surprise, I found they skip over them. As you might expect I have asked thousands of people in organizations the kind of book they would like to see on the topic of dealing with difficult people. They left very little to my imagination. Their advice:

1. If there is a principle, state it!
2. Make the words come alive. Write simply. We're easily bored.
3. Don't stretch it out. We're busy. We're also intelligent. We can understand the first time. So don't overkill.
4. Talk in the first person. Use "I." Don't use phrases like "the present author," or "the writer of this book."
5. Don't use "his/her." But don't use one rather than the other either. Alternate using *he* in some places and *she* in others.
6. Never forget who you're writing for—for people in organizations, people who are out there making a living on the front lines of life.
7. Above all, don't inject those silly illustrations involving "Paul and his secretary" or "Dr. Smith and his client." Again, we're smart. We can understand a principle without wading through endless illustrations.
8. Don't overqualify everything. We know it's hard not to talk about people without using the words "possibly" and "perhaps." But remember, those words take the power out of your writing.

My Response

When thousands of people tell you the same thing, you take them seriously. Accordingly, I've tried to incorporate all eight of their bits of advice. Specifically:

1. There are many principles. I label them clearly. There should be no mystery as to what they are.
2. Making words come alive is nothing more than revision. I've engaged in several. I consider myself an alive person and I like to write that way. I hope you agree.
3. Overkill is not one of my problems. I err on the side of writing too little. This forces me to go back and add material that is needed. Rarely—I hope never—do I rant.

4. I have no problem using "I." It appears where appropriate. When it doesn't appear, you still know I am the author of the words. I too dislike words like "it is the author's opinion." You won't see them in my writing.
5. The gender problem is always with us. So I've taken the advice. I have alternated using his and her. Don't count them, however. I may have something less than 50% in each category.
6. I never lost sight of the fact that I was writing for organizational people. That includes most of us. What I avoided, for example, was advice on how to deal with your love and/or sex problems or how to raise your children. This is not to say the information contained in this volume is not widely applicable. It is!
7. Concerning boring illustrations, let me say this. I dislike them too. They bog down progress in reading. Additionally, I have two problems with them: First, they seem unreal. Life doesn't seem to unfold the way they are written. Secondly, I have to wonder if some of them are true. There is no guarantee that I will not occasionally lapse into one myself. It's just that I have kept them to a minimum.
8. Overqualifying is not a problem with me. I agree, it dilutes the prose. So, let's leave it at this. We all know that nothing is entirely generalizeable, that every thing, every principle, has its limitations.

On Abbreviations

Throughout this book, I'll refer to Difficult—if not Impossible—people as DPs. Specifically:

DP = difficult person

DPs = difficult people

DP's = the difficult person's (possessive)

DPs' = the difficult people's (possessive)

2
On Recognizing a DP
When You See One

If you have a DP in your life right now—and you do—you don't need me to tell you.

Sometimes we have one but that fact hasn't really hit us yet. So here are the guidelines told to me by my sample of 110,000.

He might be a DP, or is becoming a DP, under any or all of these conditions:

There's a pattern of behavior. DP behaves like a DP predictably and often. It's not a once-in-a-while thing. It's their #1 characteristic—constancy. We all have our moments of stupid, asinine, unfair, prejudiced behavior. These and more. Call it the error factor, or simply our imperfections that seem to jump out now and then. That kind of behavior is normal. It is definitely not normal if it goes on and on.

We think of them often. When you find your thoughts being occupied by someone—especially if those thoughts tend on the negative side—put it down as a bad indication. It is characteristic of DPs that we think about them—and their unacceptable behavior—often. Far too often.

"It can't go on"! Now we go one step further. We begin to wonder: "How long can I survive under these conditions?" You have reached the point where you finally admit something must be done. You don't know exactly what. You are convinced only that there is no way you can survive given the poor quality of your relationship with this person.

You see your emotional health deteriorating. It's no longer an idle concern. You've upgraded the situation to critical. You're not thinking clearly. You see the quality of your life on the job—or off—disintegrating. Your relationship with this person has gone well beyond unsatisfactory. You feel you can no longer cope. Your happiness quotient is suffering.

Ordinary methods of coping have failed. The things you learned in your interpersonal communication course have been applied. No success. The "Yes-response" tactic didn't make a dent. Then you tried to reason with him. Somebody once told you that was the answer. It wasn't. Finally you tried the opposite approach. Reflect on what hasn't worked. Then do the direct opposite. That too ended in a lack of resolution. You decide that most of the ordinary approaches you've been taught don't work. They don't work because DPs aren't ordinary.

Your performance begins to suffer. The most representative case is on the job. If you type, you find yourself making more errors. You may not have the quality any more. Every aspect of your work that can get worse does.

You tense up at the mere mention of her name. You're in a reasonably good mood. Then her name is brought up. That's all it takes. Negative thoughts spew forth in rapid succession. You say to yourself, or to the guilty person, "Why did you have to bring up her name?" It may take several minutes, or hours, to get yourself together again.

You consider leaving. It's inevitable. We run out of reasonable solutions. What have we left? We can always leave—quit, transfer, walk out! In the typical life situation we aren't very serious. But with this particular person it's different. He may cause us to consider leaving more seriously.

You dread being in his presence. It's more than simply being uncomfortable. You hate it. You'd rather be anywhere else. You find yourself unnerved, stressed out, whenever you're around him. In a real way, just seeing him spoils your day.

You avoid her. You see her coming, you walk the other way. If you know she'll be somewhere, you go out of your way not to be there. Life turns into a cat-and-mouse game. You're always on the lookout. And you try to outguess her.

You hold secret meetings. You're afraid to talk to others openly about him, so you set up meeting places where you won't be seen. The implication is that if he sees you talking he'll assume it's about him. And you'll pay.

You're entertaining bizarre ideas. Things have gotten so bad that you're resorting to bizarre—unorthodox—solutions to get this person in line. Representative ideas: anonymous letters, framing the DP, entrapment, and kidnapping his kids—or at least making the threat. I have found that when conditions become intolerable humans will resort to anything to alleviate them.

3
Why DPs Treat You the Way They Do

The reasons are varied. And DPs aren't afraid to admit to them. When I talked to them, one factor stood out in bold relief. They're giving you bad treatment because of complaints they have with you. Not with the world in general, but specifically with you. You have to understand the DP's mentality if you are going to be successful at fighting back. Here they are, from the mouths of *the DPs themselves!*

1. *They don't trust you.* It's difficult to appear trustworthy even when we are. Chalk it up to the immense complexity of human relationships. So it's easy to look like we're doing something wrong, even if we aren't. On the other hand, maybe we have done something to earn DP's distrust. For whatever reasons, DP sees you as someone who is not to be trusted. That's good enough for him. His solution is to make you pay. Some classic acts that suggest distrust:

- Being caught discussing DP, negatively.
- Not supporting DP when support was needed.
- A sneaky non-verbal appearance.
- Reports from others that you are one not to be trusted.
- Failing to have a communicative relationship with DP.
- Never coming around.
- Secretly plotting (your cover was blown).

2. *They lack conflict-resolution skills.* DPs admit to a deficit when it comes to ironing out human relations problems with peers, bosses, or subordinates. Their college course in organizational conflict was a failure. Most of their attempts at being reasonable likewise have come to naught. So they resort to unsane, unreasonable, or questionably humane methods. In their words, it's the only way they know to resolve serious problems with people—at least some people.

3. *They were impressed by defective models.* Somewhere along the line we all found someone to emulate, to copy. A great statesman, senator, or movie star. If we copied the behavior of someone who was a DP the results are predictable. This is exactly what some DPs have done. They may have had a favorite grandfather who verbally battered everyone in sight. That was his style. Now it is DP's style too.

4. *First frame myopia.* If the first important encounter DP has with you leaves her negatively impressed, that may be all that is needed. From that point on, it may well be harsh treatment for you. In perception theory it's called primacy. Simply put, it's the effect of first impressions. Everyone is not unduly affected by first impressions. Some DPs are. To them, you will never be any better than that first encounter. It wasn't good, they think. They conclude that you are unworthy of good treatment.

5. *They consider you too—.* If you have too much of anything some people will make you pay. It comes down to the haves vs. the have-nots. Take beauty, for example. DP may see you as too beautiful. You don't deserve to be that beautiful. That's their justification for the way they treat you.

Of course you may be too ugly. Same reasoning. Same treatment. One of the frequently mentioned things you can be too much of was too fat. Many DPs feel that overly fat people are not entitled to anything resembling decent treatment. It's just a thing with them. They referred to them as "That fat S.O.B."!

What else can you be too much of? The list seems never to end. The big ones:

- Rich
- Popular
- Sweet
- Bright
- Well-liked

Finally, the biggest of them all: old. Age discrimination. Very prevalent among DPs—whatever their own age. In fact, the extent of age prejudice I found among everyone—DP or not—was overwhelming. I conclude that the nation's attempts to solve the problem have been signally unsuccessful. In fact, the situation is clearly worsening!

6. *It's DP's way of legally disposing of you.* DP reasons as follows: If you make a person miserable long enough eventually they'll leave. In the process DP will not have violated any law. So you will have no recourse. Nothing she has done could possibly be described as illegal. Trashy; yes: but illegal—No!

7. *They think you don't pull your weight.* Particularly in organizations, people watch one another carefully. You have to. There's too much going on. If you don't keep updated you may find yourself in the out-group, or worse.

Many of us are irritated when we see someone being paid well for doing what amounts to nothing. That someone may be a perfect bluff. But DP is on to the game and wants it ended. His assumption is that lazy people are not entitled to the normal courtesies of organizational life. Nor do they deserve fair treatment. Therefore, they must pay. And pay they do!

8. *You disobeyed.* DP wanted you to go for coffee. You didn't go. It may not have been an outright refusal, but it amounted to the same. Human relationships at any level—boss, subordinate, among peers, friends—involve thousands of requests of others. We honor some. We refuse some. The repercussions for not complying are typically minimal.

With DPs it's a different story. He is incensed. You let him down. In the process—he thinks—you also embarrassed him. As a consequence of all this you are about to get it good and hard.

Other instances:

- You resisted sexual advances (some DPs see that as disobeying).
- You were given a project. You failed to complete it. Worst, you offered no excuse.
- You were given a direct order. You failed to take it seriously.

9. *You are thought to be undeserving.* You have rank, position, power, or money. What does DP think of all this? Not much. She reasons simply that you may have it but you came about it

through shady ways. In effect, you do not deserve what you have. In fact she can name any number of people who are much more deserving than you. Her solution?

The hate treatment. "Undeserving people are entitled to nothing less."

10. *You're a failure.* If you fail at anything, some people consider you a failure across the board. DP observes that you don't measure up on some task. You botched something. Enough! DP now has you categorized as a failure. Stand by for massive doses of venom. The fact that you do many things well matters little. For him it is enough that you messed up on this one item.

Some DPs consider you a failure if:

- You're caught cheating on your income tax.
- You are arrested for a misdemeanor or felony, even though you are not convicted.
- You blow a major deal—fail to close a big sale.
- You get divorced.
- You don't want to be promoted.
- You didn't go to college.

11. *Jealousy.* Don't underestimate it. I now believe it to be one of the biggest reasons that DPs engage in their difficult behavior. It's something we rarely talk about. We just feel it in the air. It is only recently that we have discovered how pervasive and insidious it is.

DPs had no compunctions in admitting to it—at least to me. Their response to it is the problem. We're all jealous now and then. This doesn't preclude our behaving as reasonable human beings. DPs have a real problem along this line. When they are jealous they find it difficult to be decent to the target person. If they can get away with it, then, they'll go into their totally impossible act.

12. *They think you've sold them out.* Have you? Again, you may have. Or you may have looked like you did. That's enough.

None of us likes to be sold out. We know it's ever a possibility. Still when it happens it isn't fun. We adjust as best we can. We try to resolve the problem with that person, but it's never easy.

DPs aren't likely to see it that way. They see it strictly as an unpardonable sin. Forgiveness is for someone else. It definitely is not their way of doing business.

13. *They feel you have a bad image of them.* The model looks like this: if you don't like me you're going to pay. DP has the distinct impression that she suffers in your eyes. The evidence may be massive or she may simply be guessing. The results are the same. You must pay for having this bad attitude. Reasonable people live with it or try healthy ways of resolving the problem. DPs don't. They love to increase your stress level to the breaking point.

14. *They feel unappreciated, unloved.* You'd expect them to feel that way, wouldn't you? Now the question is this: Are they unappreciated because they are DPs or did they become a DP because they found out they were unappreciated? No easy answer to this chicken-egg story. From talking to them I see it this way. They never were appreciated or loved from Day 1. Their way of coping became hostile behavior—some of them, not all of them.

15. *They've never learned to be nice.* Do you know someone who can never do or say anything nice to people? Wonder why? Why must they ever be negative? Why can't they congratulate you on a job, an award, a recognition?

My answer: it is simply the way their conditioning took them. It's too complicated to unravel. Besides, it really doesn't help us that much to find out the root sources of their behavior, even if we could.

9

Some DPs can't be nice. Can't do the little nice things we all do for one another. They choose to be plain awful.

16. *Displacement.* If you can't take it out on the person to blame, take it out on whoever is handy. That's what displacement is all about. The boss is an idiot. We want to fight back. We can't. If we do we may be unemployed. So we take it out on our husband, children, the dog, the saleslady.

4
How DPs Get Away With It

How *do* they get away with it? Because we let them! We let them because we don't understand them. We don't know how to confront them. *We lack personal communicative power.*

I've talked to hundreds of DPs. I've asked them lots of embarrassing questions. Like this one: "How, in the age in which we live, do you expect that people will take the kind of stuff you dispense? How do you figure you can get away with it?" What follows are the answers they gave me. It's an important section of this book. It gives you insight into the mentality of DPs. What you begin to see is that DPs don't treat everyone alike. They have psyched *you* out and feel confident that they can push *you* around, one way or another. Here's what they told me:

You can be bluffed. DP is playing a game called "I'm a DP." She is successful in playing it because she knows you can be bluffed right out of your socks. She has you psyched out. She knows who she can and who she cannot bluff. You're one that can be bluffed, she thinks. You won't fight back.

You fear him. For whatever reasons you have a fear response whenever DP does his number on you. How it developed is not of much consequence. The fact is it's your typical response in the presence of this DP. It's exactly what the word says: *fear.* Fears tend to render us immobile. We don't fight back. That's what DP is banking on.

You have a behavioral deficit. DP feels you won't fight back because you have a communication problem. Like stuttering or shyness. Or she feels you lack the ability to talk under stressful conditions. Since about a third of Americans are thought to be shy, she may be right. At any rate, her previous experience with you confirms that fact that you don't seem to have the communicative abilities to do much of anything about the kind of treatment she is according you.

You lack courage. Similar to the items above but different in some very important ways. A lack of courage suggests a lack of belief in one's powers. Intellectual powers, physical powers, reasoning powers. Or we just feel that we'd lose if we stood up to DP. Self-esteem is the key. If we have it, we'll be inclined not to take DP's guff. If we don't, we'll let ourselves be trampled over.

Others will support them, not you. DPs feel that if things get bad you will have the support of few people—if any. They're quite convinced they'd get the lion's share of the support. With this attitude they feel they can treat you however they wish.

They can wear you down. Remember that famous Latin phrase *Illigitimi non carburundum.* English equivalent: Don't let the bastards wear you down. DPs take that idea seriously. Again, in psyching you out they have observed that you have a tendency not to fight back. So they keep up their outpouring of nonsense. It never ends. Soon, they hope, they will have slowly bludgeoned you to death. You'll surrender and leave.

You lack personal power. Back to the underlying theme of this book—that personal power is the only real power. Ultimately it's what turns the tide in dealing with DPs. It's the only thing they understand. Now when they assess you as a person lacking in personal power—right across the board—they have you. They can and will treat you however they wish, and get away with it. Not once, but all of the time. You are, they reason, defenseless!

You lack a power base. It pays to have friends, lots of them. If you have none or only a few friends then you don't have much of a power base. In any organization people are watching to see who's in whose coalition. There's nothing wrong with this. In fact, it is to be encouraged. The more friends you have the more leverage you have. DP, at the moment, sees you as a loner. Or they see you as spending your time with people who are as unpowerful as you are. You are, in their opinion, vulnerable.

You need them more than they need you. One of the worse positions to be in. Whenever someone doesn't want or need you, you're in a one-down position. They feel they have the power to do anything to you, and will. They'll treat you shabbily, disgrace you, ignore you, strip your rights from you—these and many other things. If you don't like it, tough. Leave!

Your position dictates that you must take their treatment. Here we encounter the sickest brand of DP known to humanity. He's the one who feels that whatever he does to you must be ingested and swallowed without complaint. If you are sexually harrassed, disgraced, made to look inferior, incompetent, or unattractive—you take it.

Why do you take it? Supposedly you feel obligated to DP for hiring you or keeping you on the payroll. It's one of the sub-types of the universal notion that if I am paying your salary then you'll do things like I want them done. No arguments please, just begin!

Things are just as bad elsewhere. DPs have told me that they get away with their treatment of you because both you and they know that wherever you go you'll run into people just like them. Doctors have said this: "If a nurse thinks I'm a DP, that might well be. But we're everywhere. She can leave here looking for paradise. She won't find it. Her fate, then, is to put up with me."

Blackmail$_1$: You owe me. DP reasons this way: "If I did a favor for you—especially a big favor—then you are obligated to take the poison I dispense. You take it because of the gratitude you have for me. Sure I'm unreasonable. That's your problem. Accept it. That much you owe me."

So much for what people owe us. The facts are these: we may owe people for lots of things. That does not include buying into their abnormal, sick, or otherwise impossible behavior. Nobody owes anyone that! *But DPs think you do.*

Blackmail$_2$: Real blackmail. I was appalled by how much real blackmail goes on in organizations and in human relationships generally. DPs freely admitted they were blackmailing someone in the organization. Here's the story.

A and B are buddies—best buddies. A tells B of some of his illegal, unethical, or otherwise impure behavior. Now A feels he and B will be eternal buddies. That's his first mistake. The day comes when they have a falling out, or they gradually drift apart. B becomes a DP in the eyes of A. Now B feels she can get away with it because A is in no position to fight it out. A, with her grim record, must accept whatever kind of punishing behavior B may have in mind. If she chooses to fight, B will "remind" her of her past. At least, this is what she thinks will happen. She chooses not to take any chances.

You asked for it. If I put a sign on me that says "Don't kick me" you probably will. It's natural, you say. So it is in much of living. There seems always to be someone out there doing something that they ought to know will lead to their being kicked.

DPs have told me that they only treat people poorly who go out of their way to ask for it. Like what?

- If you ask people if you are charming, or handsome, or witty, don't expect them to answer Yes. They feel that if you ask dumb questions you are asking for it. You deserve whatever you get.
- If you habitually do things that irritate others, expect sooner or later they will pull that rug out from under you. They feel that if you are so dense not to understand the consequences of your actions, then you deserve to get it good and hard.
- If you play the clown, make unkind statements about yourself, don't be surprised when someone agrees with you. Again, what did you expect?

They're so attractive you'll live with it. Yes, there really are DPs who feel they are so attractive that you'll take anything they hand out—and love it. Some feel they are terribly attractive physically. So much so that you can't resist. Even when they walk all over you, you adore them. If only you can be near them. Others feel they have so much charisma, or power, or position that you will take anything if only you can sit at their feet. And so it goes. "I'm so great I can get away with anything." That's their message. Unfortunately, your message to them is too often, "You're right"!

"I'm not doing anything illegal, so what's your problem?" If there's one line DPs repeat, that's it. Time and again they ask if their treatment of someone is illegal. I never answer that question. What they'd love me to say is "No, there is nothing illegal about it. So, you must be OK." I refuse to. For while it may not be illegal, it surely is unnecessary, inhumane, and unproductive.

"You bring out the worst in me." Here DP feels he is basically an OK person with everyone, except you. You're the one who pushes all of her wrong buttons.

Pushing DP's wrong buttons unleashes the monster in them. It brings out all of their suppressed bad traits. So it really isn't their fault at all that they treat you so lousy. It's yours.

How They Get Away with It: Final Observation

When you reflect on the above you can't help but be impressed with the idea that DPs do not engage in unacceptable behavior with everyone. You are singled out for one or more of these stated reasons. You need this information in preparing to confront the DP in your life. Be sure to think through each item to see if it fits in your case. Then when you finally confront DP you will want to discuss these possibilities. You're looking for ways to resolve the problem. It begins with understanding how DPs think.

5
Personal Communicative Power: The One Thing DPs Understand

Everyone has his own idea of what power is. For years I had mine too. Now I have data. I have what thousands have told me what, to them, powerful people do. I present those findings here just about as they were told to me. This, then, is what powerful people do, according to my cross section of 110,000 people.

They risk more. How much more? Lots more! Of the truly 25% of the people I talked to whom I considered powerful virtually everyone had this characteristic: they weren't afraid to risk. Lots has been written on this topic to be sure. Much of the words can be reduced to the idea that intelligent risk is the element that divides the more productive and happy people from the rest of us.

In the case of dealing with DPs, it translates into our not being afraid to express feelings, to disagree, to question—and not to fear the consequences. It suggests that the conservative, I-bet-only-on-sure-things philosophy, is inappropriate in today's market.

They ask for better deals. Truly powerful people are not afraid to ask for more and/or better. They've learned that it is amazing what you can get in life by simply asking.

Confronting that DP is a good example of asking for a better deal. You don't like the one you're getting now. So, in effect, your entire presentation, your case, is telling DP that you want things to get better.

They never play the helpless game. They know that there are few people who are going to do your thing for you! You have to do it yourself. If a DP is doing them in, they don't ask someone, or some group, to handle it. They fight back themselves. They may not have the skills to turn DP completely around, but they're willing to learn as they go.

They don't "hope for the best." Hopes and dreams are a big part of life—in their place. When it comes to working with DPs, action is needed. The weak mope and complain. Because they discuss DPs with other people they delude themselves into thinking they are doing something about them.

Powerful people are action-oriented. They do. They confront. They work on their relationships, always with an eye to improving them.

Some of the routine hopes of less-than-powerful people:

- DP will die
- Or have a massive heart attack.
- DP will change for the better. Just give him time.
- Things are bound to get better around here. It'll all work out.
- Somebody is bound to do something about it.

They challenge assumptions. In most of the important situations of life people are assuming this and that. The powerful assume nothing, or very little. Their standard operating behavior is to test assumptions, to challenge them. While others are taking everything at face value, the powerful wonder. They have their doubts. They will have to be shown more, a lot more.

What we think is going on is one thing. It may not be, or it may be only to some degree. What others want us to think is yet another thing. Three questions help when examining the assumptions that others want us to swallow without an argument: (1) Why is he telling me this? (2) How does he know? and (3) What is he leaving out? When you answer these, you have pretty well broken the assumption barrier!

They initiate. What do they initiate? Everything! They initiate meetings with DPs. They bring up issues, particularly touchy issues. They are the first to express an opinion. Some sit around looking at one another. The powerful move!

They greet you before you greet them. Offer their hand. Ask you a question.

The powerful aren't shy. They believe that to get anything done you have to take that first step.

They tell you where they stand. In a world of beating around the bush, the powerful stand out in bold relief as people who take a stand. It isn't necessarily a hard stand or an unpopular stand. It's just a stand. The model is "This-is-what-I-believe" and "This-is-why-I-believe-it."

They look at the people they are talking to. Some people are afraid to look you in the eye. No power there. Others look you in the eye some of the time. More power.

Truly powerful people look at you all of the time. By all I don't mean they have a stareout contest with you. They glance away for a second or two. Then they are right back to looking at you.

We don't know why this is so powerful. When you ask a lot of people the agreement is total. Everyone wants to be looked at. Everyone thinks it is one of the marks of a person endowed with power.

Looking at people implies:

- I do not fear you.
- I am not intimidated by you.
- I want to influence you.
- I am a direct and communicative person.
- You are an important person.

Not looking at the person we are trying to influence implies:

- I am weak.
- I do not have the courage of my convictions.
- I am afraid of you.
- I am intimidated by you.

They are not afraid of emotion. Powerful individuals don't come across as robots. Inside them are the same emotions that we all feel: anger, jealousy, fear, love. Additionally, they fully realize that it is normal to have a range of emotions during the course of a day, week, month. Further, they are not afraid to deal with emotion, and emotional issues.

Logic is great. The only problem with it is that emotion drives our life much more of the time. Logically we should like someone. But our emotions tell us that we don't. Logically, DP is treating us in counterproductive ways. On the emotional level DP is jealous of us. So it goes.

In any confrontation with DPs, feelings must be expressed. Weak people inhibit their expressions. The powerful feel quite at home discussing them.

They are not hung up on perfection. The powerful make mistakes and try to profit from them. They don't wait until all the evidence is in. It never is. They aren't afraid of looking silly, of erring. They know life is full of errors, of saying the wrong thing, of doing the wrong thing. They accept this, and press on.

The powerful:

- Realize that they always need more time. It's just that they can't afford it.
- Never have all the evidence they need. Nobody ever did. They're willing to go with a good case as opposed to that perfect case.

The weaker:

- Need more time.
- Need more evidence.
- Aren't quite ready.
- Are not quite in the best position yet.

They are aware of what's going on. Mindless behavior. It's the foremost enemy of us all. Call it automatic behavior if you wish. The powerful zero in on life. They are aware. They evaluate the world—especially the behaviors of the people who are determining their destiny in life: the boss, subordinates, peers, friends, relatives, family members. They're ever watching and thinking:

- What's going on here?
- What does it really mean?
- What do they want me to think it means?

These are the questions they ask. They are not about to let their lives fall victim to mindlessness. The mindless do these things:

- You cut in front of them at a checkout and they take it. When you ask them Why? they answer in mumbles and statements like "I just thought. . . ."
- They have to be hit over the head to realize something that is happening that perceptive people have known for weeks.

They don't buy the Nice Guy/Nice Gal routine. The world has oversold this idea. And *we* have overbought it. The idea is that to succeed in life you must always be a nice guy or nice gal. On the surface, it looks harmless if not downright appealing. How can anyone argue with it?

The problem is that it has very little to do with your basic humanitarian qualities, or your attitude toward your fellow humans. What it means to most people is that you are a nice guy so long as you do whatever they want you to do.

I'm terribly nice—*if* I never question you, turn you down, say Maybe, or say No. The minute I do any of these things, then I have lost that wonderful quality I once had. That's their story, at any rate.

Powerful people know when to say No! They know also when to say Yes. They will say either depending on a host of factors. Once they decide which course of action to take, they move!

The interesting thing about these people is that they can say No very nicely. They say it and we still respect them. We continue to accord them high credibility.

They are willing to fight for what they want. Powerful people see life as a good, healthy, positive fight. They see very little good happening without expending a lot of effort. If a DP gets them over a barrel, they fight back. Their attitude can be summarized this way:

- Don't hold back.
- Give everything that is important your best shot.
- Don't stand still—Move!
- Always be on the offensive.
- Give others the distinct impression that you will come roaring back.

They are not easily embarrassed. Their capacity for dissonance, for conflict, controversy or anxiety is high. They recognize that many of our relations with others can be anxiety-producing, embarrassing.

They buy the fact that things can get pretty embarrassing. What they don't buy is avoiding those situations.

Avoiding anxious situations is the calling card of the shy, the weak, the less-than-powerful.

The powerful reason like this. If I avoid potentially embarrassing situations, then I'll avoid most of the important episodes of life. If I avoid confronting DPs, for example, then the day will come when I will pay. I'll pay by becoming more and more unhappy, not getting a promotion, or more pay, or more of anything in life. I may even lose a lot of things I already have. So I must confront DPs. I must confront life. The alternative? What alternative?

They know their communicative rights. One of the enemies of personal power is that we have a dulled perception of our communicative rights.

Our communicative rights include these:

- What I can say to another person.
- How I can say it.
- How I can look when it is said (body action).
- What I can ask them and get away with.
- What I can demand of them.

When you deal effectively with a DP you must know what you can say and cannot. Powerful people know what they can say. The rest of the world is still wondering.

They anticipate negative situations. Life, at times, seems to repeat itself. People ask the same questions. They choose the same kinds of entertainment.

There is repetition in behavior toward us too. We hear the same cutting, sarcastic remarks predictably from time to time. Acts of rudeness and aggressiveness can be plotted with accuracy.

When they occur the weak remain at a loss for what to say, what to do. The powerful are ready. They know that it is hard to come up with immediate responses in sticky situations. So they prepare themselves. The responses they provide in these situations look spontaneous. Actually they are well planned.

They evaluate group pressure. The weak succumb to group pressure. They are ready to drop whatever they are doing and go along with others. It's all done in a rather mindless way.

The powerful, when subjected to the same pressures, evaluate them. They rarely automatically respond to anything. They take appropriate time. Then they make a decision. Sometimes they join in; other times they resist.

Since they have a good opinion of themselves (self-esteem) they do not measure their success in life by the approval they receive from others. They'd like approval. It's just that realism tells them it's not practical to expect it always.

They get lots of feedback, and they evaluate it. I estimate that about 1% of the world gets massive feedback during a lifetime. The rest don't push for it. And since there are few who will volunteer to give it to them, they go without it.

Those who have evolved into powerful individuals routinely ask for feedback. Then they do what most of us fail to do: they process it. They are not in a hurry to change their behavior until they see the whole picture. To do otherwise would be to take on every new day with a new personality. They ask these questions of themselves and of the feedback that others have provided:

- Does it square with my perceptions of myself?
- Is it a minor flaw that really makes little difference to anyone?
- Am I fully aware of this characteristic?
- What good would come from my omitting this item from my repertoire of behaviors?
- Would I be comfortable with this new behavior?
- Is this behavior a big part of my personality, part of the me that differentiates me from all others?

They like themselves. Powerful people have a healthy self-concept. In a real sense, they like their own value systems. They also feel that they have a good attitude toward themselves and others.

They are rarely down on themselves. Consequently they have few problems with depression. In brief, they know who they are, what they stand for—and they like it.

They are not easily impressed. They listen, they attend, they ponder, reflect and evaluate. Through all of this they maintain a positive attitude. That doesn't mean that they are taken in by what they hear and see. Quite the contrary.

They are never in a hurry to believe when the stakes are high. They are unwilling to stake their destinies on what you say. They believe more in behavior, much more. They want to watch you. Especially do they want to see if what you say coincides with what you do.

They're cautious when it makes sense to be cautious. They see life as having too much deception and dishonesty for them to be easily impressed.

They work at being a person of fair play. At another point in this book I state that a lack of fair play is one of the most serious conditions facing the world. I suggest further that it is easy to be perceived as not being a person who regularly engages in fair play. That's why the powerful among us go out of their way at being a person noted for fair play. It takes effort, lots of it.

Everything they do is first evaluated—yes, even automatically evaluated—from this point of view: will it be fair to all concerned? It's a tough assignment for all of us. The powerful succeed to a remarkable degree.

6
Your Behavior Must Be Likeable, Even to DPs

Likeable behavior is not a secret of life. There are no secrets to life. It's just one of those priceless ingredients that tends to get us more of everything.

Put it this way. Does unlikeable behavior get us very far? Nobody ever answers Yes!

There isn't an awful lot to say. Likeable behavior is just plain being nice. It means not aggravating people when you can avoid it. It means being soft on the other person.

When I asked my sample what kinds of behaviors were likeable there were few surprises. Here's what impressed them most.

1. *Paying close attention to people.* It's powerful and it's likeable. You're on their wave length. You're listening—hard! You respond with meaningful, relevant responses. That's one way they know you have been listening to them closely.

Ask people how many people in their lives so far have a reputation for paying close attention to them. They initially think many but they end with only one or two names. It's not one of the better things we do when we interact with one another.

When you pay close attention to people they feel like:

- What they are saying is important to you.
- You are trying to understand them.
- You feel there are other ways of seeing the world.
- You are open-minded.
- You are willing to learn.
- You don't have all the answers.

2. *Positive nonverbals.* Put briefly, the world doesn't need another grim looking person! Even negative people enjoy people who look reasonably positive.

The most frequently mentioned (and appreciated) positive nonverbals:

- Smiling, at least some of the time.
- Posture that looks like you want to be there.
- Looking at the other person.
- Looking at the other person as though you liked her.
- Not being afraid to gesture.
- Relaxed posture.

3. *Meshing ability.* Discussed also in Chapter 8, meshing involves talking some and listening some and moving from one to the other smoothly.

4. *Being appropriately brief.* There's a place for longer utterances and a place for briefer responses. Most people enjoy relatively short speeches and responses. Some call this making the minimum effective response. A request for the correct time need only bring a few seconds reply. We don't need an oration on how time slips away.

5. *Displaying ignorance.* In an age in which everyone is supposed to know everything few of us like to admit to ignorance. On the surface that sounds reasonable. From another point of view it isn't.

Ignorance means we don't have all the answers. You have a problem. I don't have the solution. I'm quite willing to admit that I don't. Life is complex. How can one person have answers to the infinite number of problems. They can't; and it's foolhardy to try.

Ignorance of this kind is likeable. Rather than play the omniscience game, we simply stop trying to fix up all of your problems. Those who do not believe in this principle are ever ready to tell you and me what we should do, ought to do. They love to jump in and fix things up—immediately.

6. *Enjoying what you are doing.* Whether giving a speech, pumping gas, or serving hamburgers, can you enjoy it? You certainly can. If this is true, why do so many people look like they are not enjoying the thing they're doing? Lots of reasons. It may well be that most people simply do not really enjoy doing anything.

If you look like you are doing it because you have to—not because you love to—you lose points on the likeability scale.

7. *Letting the other person win some encounters.* The tendency to one-up is a characteristic that people intensely dislike. When you one-up someone you have a better answer—you think. Your example tops theirs. Your experience is vastly superior to theirs. No matter what they say, you refute it. It's most definitely unlikeable behavior.

Likeable people aren't concerned with winning every encounter with you. They may know more than you, but they don't hold it over you. They let you err without making a scene.

8. *Rewarding behavior.* Rewarding behavior is giving behavior. You do things for people. You give them material things. You say nice things to them, things you genuinely feel. When you compliment someone you are engaging in rewarding behavior.

The reasons for not complimenting someone are well known. They already know it; I'll be embarrassed; they'll be embarrassed; it won't come out right; they'll think I'm after something. None of these excuses is worth the paper it is written on. We need, we appreciate, compliments. We love people to tell us we are doing well or that we are appreciated.

Have you noticed that there are some people who never compliment anyone? They seem unable to say anything nice to anyone. There are plenty of them out there. We can have compassion for these people for they tend to be disliked. Look at the people who aren't afraid to give you positive feedback. You'll find most of them to be liked by virtually everyone.

9. *Engaging in normal life courtesies.* It may not seem obvious to us, but the normal courtesies of life are not outmoded. Opening a door for someone—young, middle aged, or older—is still appreciated. Talking one at a time, not interrupting someone, saying "Thank You." They're all very much alive and appreciated.

The macho age (or macha—the female equivalent) is no longer in style. In fact, it never was!

10. *They talk as a human being—not as a role.* Your attorney no doubt talks to you like attorneys talk to people! Most doctors behave the same way. They talk to you like a doctor talking to a patient. And so it goes. We talk like our role, not as human beings.

Talking as one human being to another is likeable. We love it. When we find it in a professional we recommend that person to our friends. It is, we think, rare. And we are right.

12. *They have a sense of humor about themselves.* They may not know the latest joke. They have something much better: a sense of humor that says "I don't take myself that seriously." When they make a mistake, they can laugh about it for they know it isn't going to be fatal. Few things ever are.

Many of life's pressing problems they smile at. They worry not that you will judge them as ineffective if they poke fun at themselves. They like themselves. So they are in a position to laugh off their errors.

We like them for it.

Summary

What of likeable behavior as we deal with DPs? It's needed there even more. DPs, too, appreciate good treatment. It doesn't mean we're weak. It means we're intelligent. It makes any encounter with a DP that much easier. And DP's response is always nicer.

7
The Excuses—Letting DPs Off the Hook

I've heard them all—the hundreds of excuses and justifications for letting DPs continue to pull us down. Not one of them makes sense. Here are the top eleven.

1. *"They'll get me."* "If I dare fight back, I'm as good as dead. He has a long memory. Somehow, somewhere, sometime I'll pay." It's an attitude that's hard to fight. How do you prove to someone that there's nothing to worry about? You don't. You just try to get them to consider the alternatives.

Few people "get" anyone today. It's too difficult. Most of us don't have that kind of power. Nor would we necessarily use it if we did. Point: If you confront DP the right way you won't have to worry about retaliation. Two more points.

First, most of us learn early in life that we can't eliminate everyone who dares to confront us. There are just too many people.

Secondly, I checked with over 600 people who had confronted one or more DPs over a six year period. One had been fired. The others couldn't recall anyone going the retaliation route. I was impressed.

Response. Do it right and you won't have to worry about retaliation.

2. *"I have no power."* They're talking about *personal communicative power.* They don't think they have any—or enough. They don't. They lack power because no one has shown them how to get it. To put it another way, they don't understand what power qualities are.

I've asked thousands. What they told me is the subject of Chapters 3 and 4. For now I can only say that they're right. Most of the people I've met really do lack power. And personal power is the name of the healthy, positive game of fighting it out with DPs.

Response. It's easier than you think to become a communicatively powerful person. You need only know what impresses and influences people, positively and negatively. Then do it.

3. *"I don't have the skills."* What skills are they talking about? Conflict resolution skills. Negotiation skills. The skills to think and talk under tough conditions.

These could have been learned in high school, or college. Unfortunately most courses devoted to conflict resolution are either too theoretical or far too oversimplified. One leaves with the feeling that problems with DPs can be solved by just remembering this one thing. What that one thing is varies across instructors. Samples: "Never confront them." "Just smile a lot." "Humor them out of it." "Use sugar instead of vinegar."

Response. You can develop communication skills the same way you can develop personal power. That's my mission in this book: to give you both.

4. *"I can't take the anxiety."* We're back to that. There's little left to be said. Except this: What are the alternatives? There are none!

Response. Anxiety is everywhere. It doesn't go away. So don't fight it; buy into it.

5. *"Yes, but not now."* Call it the procrastinator in us. There's always a better time when we'll be better prepared. Or we'll be in a better mood. Or our throat will be clearer.

We're not ready; they're not ready. Sure it's got to be done. The question is when? The answer is not now.

Response. It's delusional thinking. Who's ever really in the mood to confront DPs. Few that I've known. So screw up your courage, set a time, and move. Otherwise things will continue on their march toward complete deterioration.

6. *"Yes, but not me."* "Let's find George and send him in there. He'll do a much better job than I. He's a great communicator, has guts, and loves confrontations."

Flawed reasoning. Flawed because the difficulties you have with DP are unique. They're the result of interactions between the two of you. Nobody understands that relationship like you do. So you can't send in somebody off the bench. Thousands have tried. The results have been predictably disappointing.

Response. If you're the one with the problem then you're the one to confront. Substitutes worsen an already strained relationship.

7. *"I'm easily intimidated."* We all are. It's just that some of us don't see intimidation as the end of life. We see it as a big part of life. Potentially intimidating people seem to be behind every bush. Our job is to press on in the face of intimidation.

Response. Intimidation is one of the dirty tricks used by DPs. Don't let it affect you in the extreme. Positive confrontation neutralizes intimidation.

8. *"I don't understand DP's mentality."* There's no reason why you should. The communication literature contains nothing on what DPs are thinking, why they behave the way they do, and how they think they can get away with it. The psychology literature is even less helpful. Freudian analyses are fun to read. It's just that they are of little practical value.

You're right! We *must* understand how DPs think. I found out by interviewing hundreds of them. It's all in Chapters 3 and 4.

Response. To succeed with a DP you study their motivations, assumptions, and the way they see life. They're complicated. But make the effort.

9. *"I don't know what I can say—and get away with."* Let's call these your communication rights. Here are the questions: Exactly what can I say to DP? In what tone of voice? Can I directly confront her with the facts, as I see them?

The answers *are* this book. It's the essence of dealing with DPs. We have to know, in other words, exactly what the parameters of power communication are. When we know them, understand them—then we're half way there.

Response. What you know about communication so far probably isn't good enough. DPs must be approached in non-traditional ways. That's one reason most people fail in their attempts to reason with them.

10. *"I'm communicatively flawed."* Here we have the most widely quoted excuse: "I have a problem that renders me ineffective." Like what? Like those mentioned earlier: "I'm shy." "I hate conflict." "I get tongue-tied." "I'm too easily intimidated." Who doesn't? Who isn't?

It's not that people aren't telling the truth when they admit to these problems. They are. My response, once again, is what are the alternatives? If we hide behind our so-called limitations then DPs continue on their destructive paths.

Response. Commit yourself to confronting DPs even though you feel you're not the best communicator on the block. It's amazing what practice will do. Jump in!

11. *"Things will get better. I'll just be patient."* I'd be surprised if they do. The number of DPs who improve simply with the passage of time approaches zero. Unless sickness or death removes them from the scene they typically get worse. I know of no born-again DPs. On the contrary. My experience leads me to conclude that with DPs it's downhill all the way.

Response. Time may cure all when our hearts are broken in romance. It cures very little in the world of DPs. That's because time is neutral. Positive action cures all—if anything does.

Breaking out of the Excuse Trap

Excuses and justifications make up a big part of life. Nobody could survive without invoking a few now and then. So we forgive others—and especially ourselves—when we come up with yet another one. That's OK—to a point. Where we have to be careful is in believing our own press releases. Is that DP likely to intimidate us to an extreme? How about the other hundred excuses we routinely embrace? Can we afford to subscribe to them, with a straight face?

We cannot. The bare bones of reality have to be faced. Consider the excuses. Then dash them on the rocks. You don't really believe them. Neither does anyone else.

The people whom I consider to be powerful rarely resort to looking for convenient justifications. It's too easy a game to play.

Their game is go for action now—that's the cash. Leave excuses for later—the credit.

8
Fighting Back:
The Method That Works

My sample of something over 110,000 working people taught me much. The most important lesson I learned was this: Don't look for simple solutions to complex problems. DPs are highly complex. It follows that there is no simplistic procedure for disarming them. The principles are simple enough; but there are several of them. But first let me review once again how I know what I think I know.

First, you find out who the difficult people are. Who is driving you crazy? What exactly is it that they do? This is the easy part. The minute you walk into an organization there are scores of people ready with their hit list of DPs. I've described the varieties of DPs in Chapter 10.

Next, what kinds of approaches meet with success? Which kinds end in failure? This was the tough part. Tough because it took so long. I had to come back to check on what people did. Did they take my advice? If so, what happened? When something obviously proved to be of no value, it was discarded. This left me with the things that worked.

Years of this kind of trial and error resulted in my seminar on Dealing with Difficult People, and this book.

Finally, there is the follow-up. Wherever I conduct my seminar (some 70,000 have attended), I always tell the participants that they are urged to call me about their problems with DPs. It's a continuing feedback system that tells me how the system is holding up. I am happy to tell you that the system, the philosophy I espouse in this book, is standing up well indeed. With the passing of each day I am more convinced that I have a powerful approach, one that has stood the test of time, one that works.

The Ground Rules

To disarm and neutralize DPs, you can't choose some of the principles and ignore others. You must buy the whole package. Then you must incorporate each into your unique communication style. What else must you do?

Practice. You probably have little experience in dealing with real DPs so you don't know what to expect. I believe your best ally is to find someone to role play with. You play yourself. Let the other person play DP. Talk about how you did. Once is never enough. Ten to a dozen will do wonders for you. Practice also dissipates stage fright, or anxiety. You'll feel calmer when you actually confront DP.

Strive to follow every principle. I have found that when you leave one or more out, the success rate goes down fast. After each encounter, go over the principles to find out if you violated any. If so, work especially hard on those items the next time.

A few of the principles—maybe many of them—may appear to be deceptively simple. They are. They're known as classic principles of power communication. They look easy. Yet they are never easy to put into practice.

Make the principles second nature. Get them into your system so that they are automatic. If you have to think about them while you are confronting DP it will detract from your performance.

Always make a thoroughgoing analysis of each encounter. You grow from reflecting on what you did well and not so well. If possible, ask DP how he felt.

Believe in yourself. Believe you are becoming a more powerful person. That's where personal power begins.

Finally, believe in the system I have evolved. I know it works. Don't fall for systems that oversimplify life and reduce approaches to two lines. Nothing important can be that simple.

The 24 Principles of Fighting It out with DPs

1. *Confront DP directly.* Personal communicative power begins with putting yourself in the presence of DP. You meet one on one, with nothing in between.

The alternatives don't work. First, we can send somebody else. The problem is that your unsatisfactory relationship with DP is a function of you and her. Nobody else can appreciate the nature of it. They cannot talk for you.

Write her a letter? I wouldn't. Letters have no power. They are easy to throw in the waste basket. They are not you. They are an abstraction of you. If they have any effect at all, it's a negative one. Since they represent one-way communication at its worse, they tend only to aggravate the person on the receiving end. That you don't need.

You could phone her. You could but—again—it's the coward's way out. It is always less than satisfactory; and the problems you have with DP are just too complex to work through on the telephone.

We're left with being there physically. Sure it can raise your level of anxiety. Just buy into the anxiety and pain.

2. *Unfurl your flag.* When you unfurl your flag (real estate term) you are honest, open. You successfully resist your desire to manipulate, to deceive that other person, in this case the DP. It takes practice. For most of us think immediately of how we are going to set up the other person. Manipulation comes naturally. Few of us dedicate ourselves to telling things as we see them.

When you unfurl your flag you gain immediate communicative power. People who do it for the first time in their lives are nothing short of amazed with the results. DPs too find it refreshing. It makes a statement about you. Most of all it is the acme of power.

3. *Mesh.* You can talk and talk. You can tell DP this and that. You can reject what DP says out of hand. You can let it pass through your ears, unnoticed. The name for that kind of behavior is non-listening. It's the world's foremost communication malady. It can be summarized by saying that nobody pays very much attention to what any one else says.

Too bad. For there is power associated with talking at the right time and then listening closely. Here's what you do in the good instance:

- You talk to DP. Hopefully, DP is listening closely.
- DP then responds with relevant statements.
- Hopefully you are listening closely to DP.

- The cycle continues. Good listening, close listening. Then come the responses: relevant observations, statements of feeling, etc.
- Each has respect for the other's communicative rights. And one of these communicative rights is the right to be taken seriously, to be listened to.

Meshing, then, says that you can't always talk. Not only must you provide time for DP to talk, you must go out of your way to listen well.

Powerful people mesh!

4. *Exchange perceptions.* To convert DP you must not only present your case, your observations, your feelings. You must give her an opportunity to tell you hers. Violate this principle and you are left with no change. DP simply becomes more infuriated with you—and with good reason.

Often we feel that we have a corner on truth, justice, and wisdom. We are so right and DP is so wrong. My experience is this: I have never known of a problem involving you and DP that was not a joint result of your interactions. You're not totally right; neither is DP. It is true that you may have contributed practically nothing to the problem between you. It may be DP's imagination. Imagination or not, he thinks you are a real part of the problem.

Let me put it this way. You can't resolve your bad relationship unless you understand fully what DP sees in your behavior. Likewise, she must know the full story from your viewpoint. Remember, your difficulties may be due to the fact that you are perceiving the same behavior in radically different ways.

5. *Dramatize, at least some of the time.* I have very little faith in ordinary talk. It's been used trillions of times, often with little success. I have much more faith in dramatization. Dealing with DP gives you a golden opportunity to paint pictures, images in his head. That's impact.

You can tell DP that your relationship is hurting. Or you can describe what happens to you as you get out of bed and head for work. That's what dramatization is all about.

Dramatization makes it easy for us to appreciate a problem. It's also much easier to listen to. Ordinary talk can be boring. Good dramatization should seldom be.

6. *Your goal is to improve the relationship, not destroy it.* Before I talk with them, many people's approach to DP is to whip up the courage, then run in and "tell him off." When I ask them how long they intend to be in the organization with DP they may say something like 30 more years. Then I ask them what kind of relationship they will have to live with for those 30 years. There is a predictable hesitation. My point is made.

The brutal facts of being alive include this one: You have to live with people whether you like them or not. So why not try to improve the relationship? Mexican standoffs make for ulcers. Mutual hate relationships—the same. We don't need them. Life is far too brief for all of that.

This leaves us with only one good option: Meet DP on his own ground with a clear goal of improving the relationship. It's the only option that makes sense both in the short and in the long runs.

7. *You can't love DPs out of it.* My system of disarming DPs involves these working assumptions. First, positive attitude is essential. Secondly, affection is a big part of life—in organization, indeed everywhere. We need both to succeed with DPs.

You can't love them out of it. Pure affection by itself won't work. It never has. Love-affection, combined with the philosophy I espouse here—that spells relief.

8. *Be firm. Don't collapse.* It's easy to fall apart in a confrontation with DPs. They tend to be tough and intimidating. That's one of the reasons they're deserving of the label DP.

Your job is to be determined and resolute. At the sign of the first sub-crisis, don't give up or run out the door. The only right attitude is this one: "I'm staying here until this thing is resolved, or at least is well on the road to resolution."

If it's your first real encounter with a DP you will likely be ready to make peace fast, at any cost. Resist it.

9. *Treat DP as you would a friend.* You may hate DP. You may feel he's emotionally disturbed and that nothing good can be said about him. You may think that, but don't act that way.

You're dealing with another human being. DP is human. He responds, as do we all, to humanity. This means we are optimally assertive. Now assertive people, by definition, treat people like this. They:

- Keep a positive attitude.
- Treat them with respect.
- Speak nicely, with positive vocal overtones.
- Engage in positive nonverbals.

Let me put it this way. I have known few people who ever got anywhere with DPs who aggressed against them. DPs are different from you and me in some respects. In others, they are the same. Like us, they respond best when treated well.

10. *Your behavior must be likeable.* My sample gave their opinions as to what constitutes likeable behavior. The results are presented in Chapter 6. Here let me deal with the topic from a slightly different point of view.

First, I'm not talking about having DP's approval for everything you do. Or going out of your way to secure his love. You don't have to be loved by him. And that's good. You're probably not. Nor do you need everyone's approval or good will for whatever you do.

You can easily engage in behaviors that most people will interpret as likeable. Elementary smiling. Avoiding the appearance of trying not to trap someone. Not shouting.

11. *Don't give in, or give up.* It's easy to give in to DP, or simply to give up. The word here is persistence. I like the word "intrepid" too. The elementary truth is that the prize most often will go to the most persistent person—when you're in a contest with a DP.

Since DP doesn't want to resolve the bad relationship between you, she will often expend a lot of her effort to bring things to a close, in a hurry. The practical consequence is that if you let her off the hook, it's back to Square 1. Nothing having been resolved, you must now begin the process over again on another day. Now you're in a weaker position. She has already stopped you dead in your tracks. Her perception of you as a person of power has diminished.

12. *Timing really is important.* DPs, like all of us, have good days and bad. They're in better moods in the morning or in the afternoon. You must know which.

Elementary horse sense comes into play at this point. For instance, it never is a good idea to approach someone when you know there is a crisis in the organization. When their world is falling apart, DPs have little time for you. The possible situations are endless. It makes good sense to work with anyone when they are at their best. Manipulation? No! It's called using your head.

13. *You must have a robust case.* Assumptions aren't good enough. Neither is what your intuition tells you. To turn DP into an ally, a supporter, you must demonstrate that serious conditions exist between the two of you. You do this by having a case—not just any case, but a *robust* case. Your case is robust when:

- You have lots of good evidence as opposed to what you believe to be true.
- Objective third parties agree that your case is convincing.

32

- You have thought through the implications for you and for DP.
- You have anticipated and are ready for the major objections to each issue you present.
- Therefore, you're not likely to be surprised by anything DP will come back with.
- You have studied the case from DP's point of view.
- You are aware of the standard excuses and justifications that DP is likely to unload on you. So you have appropriate and reasonable responses to them.
- You have thought through several acceptable solutions.

14. *Don't block all exits.* DP needs room to negotiate. So do you. This is best accomplished by your assuming that she can and may well be right about some things. An attitude of allness, in other words, causes her to harden her stance. Think about it. Is there nothing right in what she is saying? Not one valid point? Are all of her arguments and points based on pure prejudice? Hardly!

An attitude of "Everything she says is stupid"! leaves her with no options. Intelligent discussion is impossible.

15. *Keep the Monkey on DP.* A monkey is something you put on someone else or take on yourself. When dealing with DPs, a monkey is your case—your *robust* case. Reduced to its lowest terms, dealing with DPs involves placing two monkeys on his back. First, what you are telling her in so many words is that she is playing a game called "I'm a DP. Secondly, your message to her is "I have no intention of playing it with you any longer."

When DP perceives what you have in mind she may take steps to end the conversation, or the encounter. How long it will be before she makes her move varies with her, you, and the situation. In other words, DP gets your message that you find her behavior unacceptable. She puts a plan of her own in effect. That plan amounts to getting you out the door as soon as possible. Why? Because DPs rarely have any desire to attempt a resolution of the problem. Again, had they, then they would have long since begun the process of negotiating with you.

The methods DP uses to get you out the door, or to shut you up, are well known. They range from "It wasn't my fault." to "Gee, I had no idea!" The complete list is found in Chapter 00.

16. *Expect positive results.* When you look like you expect people to treat you well they tend to. Tons of research has shown up in the journals and textbooks in the last twenty years. The message is clear. People who look positive, who act positive, and who expect that DP will respond positively are always more successful than their opposites.

There's a footnote to it all. Your positiveness must include an attitude of acceptance of DP. If he thinks you don't accept him as a human being he will normally retreat back into his DP behavior.

One of the most frequently asked questions is this: "How can I look accepting of someone when in fact I can't stand him?" The answer lies in the phrase *Drop it!* Bad feelings for anyone can literally be dropped from your system. You need only practice.

You're in Houston's international airport. You find your flight will be delayed six hours. You have several alternatives. One, you can fret, pace the floor, play the game of Ain't it Awful, followed by I'll-Never-Fly-this-Airline-Again.

There's a better alternative. You can drop that bad emotion and accomplish all kinds of things. This includes taking a walk, writing letters, reading, thinking up solutions to problems—in short, all kinds of productive things.

Can you learn to drop bad emotion and get on with productive ventures? Sure. It takes a little practice. After a few trial runs you'll amaze yourself with how easy it is.

So it is with DPs. You can learn to drop bad emotion—at least during the confrontation—and treat DP in accepting ways.

What happens when your attitude is one of rejection? Lots of predictable things. The biggest thing is that DP begins to treat you the same way. That's right, we tend to treat others as they treat us. So with a mutual dislike attitude, nothing very constructive is likely to result.

17. *Go out of your way to be an accurate communicator.* Notice that this principle does not say that you should be an accurate communicator. It says *Go out of your way!* Why? First, I am quite convinced that it is easy to become a sloppy communicator. We exaggerate, overgeneralize, forget about the limitations, deal in heresay, half-truths, gossip. And that's just the beginning. To overcome these natural inclinations we have to put extra effort into how we communicate.

Take a close look at the case you have against DP. Let's say you feel you are chronically treated in an unfair manner. Do you have clear evidence that this is the case? Or are you relying on what your friends have told you? Has DP treated you fair in anything? Probably. Are you going to admit it? You should.

Do you have weaknesses, loopholes in your case? Most of us do. In fact, I have found nobody to have an airtight case against anyone in my work in organizations.

If we act as though there are flaws in our evidence, our arguments, our issues—we gain respect. People, including DPs take us more seriously. They know, as do we all, that nobody has a corner on truth. Reasonable people have never claimed otherwise.

18. *Let DP maintain his face.* Don't expect he will admit to being stupid, unfair, undemocratic, or inhumane in his treatment of you. To do so would be tantamount to admitting he is really an inferior human being.

DP feels he is OK and you had better treat him that way too. When you let him save his face you are honoring the oldest contract in human relations. That contract says that you must allow me to act out my role. Whatever I present myself as, you must not blow the whistle on me. You must never show me out to be an imposter, a bluff, a fake, even if you think I am.

Violate this contract and you may as well have stayed home!

19. *Get off the self-righteousness streetcar.* "I am very, very right. You are very, very wrong." That's the message of the self-righteous. Sound familiar? It should. Some people make a religion out of it. Others of us fall into it now and then.

It's rarely a good medicine for anyone; and it never cures. What actually happens is that it causes DP to further entrench himself in his position. Why? Because he and we both know that it is contrary to all we know about human relationships.

To be right about everything is a delusion that foolish people cling to. Intelligent people know that we can only be right, or wrong, to some degree.

The self-righteous are extremists. Being unwilling to admit that they could be wrong, they dig bigger and bigger holes for themselves. In the end, they are rejected out of hand as infantile.

20. *Ask for changes that are possible.* You may want DP to undergo a complete change of personality. He can't. There's no use asking for this, even if you dared.

Concentrate on the doable. DP can certainly alter many of her behaviors toward you. She can cease doing things that make for very bad relations. There are many things we can all do.

What we can't do is the impossible.

21. *Push hard for feedback.* DP has lots of feelings toward you. Find out what they are. The more you know the better you can map out a mutually acceptable solution. But DP is no different than the rest of the world in that respect: He is reluctant to give you negative feedback. So you have to push.

When you first ask DP for feedback you tend to get none. Or you get some vague thoughts about your behavior. Don't take it. Ask for more. Ask for greater specificity. When you follow this procedure she typically breaks down. Now you are moving.

To know what DP dislikes about you, how he sees you as contributing to the mutual problem, is the biggest leap you will take. It gives you the stuff to make changes with. You know that if there is to be a satisfactory solution you'll have to make some changes yourself.

22. *Make a contract for improved behavior.* Salespeople call it asking for the sale. It means that you are going to ask DP for specific behavioral changes. It means also that you are prepared to tell DP what you intend to do to make the new relationship work.

It's the final step. If you leave without a contract you'll always be vague about what is expected of each other.

23. *Let DP know you will be back.* It's an interesting factor in human relations. People who confront DPs and then never return tend to have a lower success rate. What DP needs to know is that you will be watching her behavior and that you will return from time to time to talk about it, to evaluate how you are both doing.

24. *Increase your communication with DP.* An even better idea is to make DP a friend. When you talk to people on a regular basis they tend to become your friend. The opposite applies too. The people we avoid, rarely talk to—these are the people we are most likely to have problems with. Communication may not be the total cure, but it's a great medicine.

9
DPs: Their Tactics and Stratagems

I've talked to hundreds of them. I told you a lot of what they told me in Chapters 3 and 4. Here I want to tell you about some of their more frequently employed tactics, their stratagems in dealing with you. By their own admission:

They aren't interested in resolving anything. Sure, it's a wide generalization, but it's a good one. If there's one thing that characterizes DPs it is that they don't want to talk with you about the problem. They have no particular desire to resolve it. If they did, they would have attempted a resolution long ago. In the typical case, they've had plenty of time.

The fact is they are quite content with things as they are. When you probe them on this they give out with a string of excuses and justifications. They don't see anything wrong with their behavior. It's all *your* fault. Notice I said it's *all* your fault. That is quite different from saying that both of you are contributing to the problem.

They see little value in discussing it. When you finally get to see DP it could be a short visit. They don't want to talk to you. Consequently, you can bet that they are going to employ tactics that are designed to collapse you before you can get started. What are those tactics? The standard ones we've read about over the years, plus a few that are idiosyncratic to specific DPs.

1. *Not now.* They never seem to have time for you. You ask if they have a minute and they say Yes, reluctantly. As soon as they know what you are up to, suddenly they've run out of time. Come back tomorrow. Or, better, next month. Come back anytime in the future, the further in the future the better. Right now? It's just not a good time.

Counter tactic: For this and all other tactics and stratagems, your Number 1 defense is *persistence.* Keep the monkey on them. Don't take it back under any circumstances, unless clearly it is the only remaining alternative.

When they tell you come back some other time, pin them down. Exactly when? And how much time will I have? These are the questions you must get straight.

When you come back, expect the same treatment. Now she has a meeting in five minutes, a report that is overdue, or she has scheduled another appointment, by mistake of course.

Press on. Is there really a cure for this kind of behavior on the part of DP? Only one. It's called "I'm going to be back until this thing is resolved." If you have that attitude, it will work for one good reason: She can't live with you on her back day in and day out. The anxiety is too great. It isn't worth it. Ultimately she will have to meet with you.

2. *Talking louder, faster than you.*

One of the oldest tactics in the history of communication. It's used to scare you out of your wits, to intimidate. DPs are often verbal. They can outtalk you by the sheer weight of their verbal output.

Loud talkers, especially, disturb our equilibrium. We're used to being around reasonable people who talk in normal conversational tones.

Counter tactic. Don't engage in a contest with DP. You'll lose. Anyway, the last thing you want to do is behave like DP.

So what do you do? You talk about their ranting and raving. You see, DP is playing a sub-game, once again. This one is called "Louder and Faster."

Since it is a game, you deal with it as you would any game. You blow the whistle on the game. In this case, you let DP know you are aware of what he is trying to do. Secondly, you inform him that you have no intention of taking it. Of course, you say this nicely and with restraint. The question is, will it work?

It will work because DP has no alternative but to ultimately behave like a reasonable human being. If you leave and nothing has been accomplished, come back. Again, sooner or later, DP won't be able to take it any longer and will calm down. Until he does, keep blowing the whistle and keep coming back.

3. *Shifting the responsibility.*

DPs rarely blame themselves for anything. That's right, they play the self-righteous game to the hilt. When they finally understand what you are saying, they go into their "Not me" routine. They—they would like you to believe—are innocent. You have a case, all right. What you must understand is that the perpetrators of this foul deed, or deeds, is out there somewhere. Surely you don't for a minute think they were responsible, do you?

Yes, you do. You are entirely convinced that the buck stops with them. You know this because you've done your homework. True, none of us knows anything in any absolute sense. Still many hours of thinking and reflection on the evidence should place the blame right at DP's door.

Counter tactic. Methodically and comprehensively reveal your case. Show how DP figures in as the central person even though others may have been obliquely involved. Above all, don't agree. If you are ready to agree, if DP convinces you, then you have committed a major blunder: you have failed to know what you are talking about. Long before the confrontation you should have ruled out all alternative explanations such as the fault lying with someone else.

4. *"How dare you question my integrity?"*

Any hint that DP has acted toward you in an unfair or chronically sleazy manner can and does cause many DPs to bristle. "Who do you think you are coming in here and laying that junk on me?" DP, in his estimation at any rate, is Simon Pure, faultless. He may have negative qualities, but the one you are hinting at certainly isn't one of them. So why don't you just leave while you are still ahead!

Counter tactic. First, be careful not to question DP's integrity. Never go beyond describing what happened and how you feel about it. If you stick with those two, he can't accuse you of character assassination. In fact, let him know that clearly you are not in the business of name-calling.

What you are in the business of is resolving conflict that involves the two of you. That should be your only concern. Realize that everyone is touchy about their image. If you suggest that DP has a tarnished image, don't expect much more to come from your discussion.

5. *Berating you.*

Most DPs I have met have a sharp tongue and they know how to use it. It's one of their standard offensive tactics. It goes like this. If DP makes you out to be an undesirable, unattractive, self-seeking sicko, then you will retreat out the door. If you leave, DP reasons he will have you off his back once again. So it's worth a try.

It's effective. Few of us are used to obscenities. Fewer of us know how to respond to someone reducing us to an absurdity. We collapse. The result is that once again DP prevails. Nothing was accomplished. It was a waste of our time. Worst, the problem remains unresolved.

Counter tactic. Blow the whistle on the sub-game. Let DP know that you are aware of what she is trying to accomplish. Then persist.

Ask for better treatment! If DP swears at you, ask him not to. Tell him you don't appreciate it and that you expect no more! And keep saying it until it ends. It really is amazing what you can get by simply asking!

6. *I'm sorry!*

DP apologizes excessively. Yes, she did these things to you. She now recognizes the error of her ways. So please forgive, and forget.

I suggest you do neither, at least until you are satisfied that she really is committed to treating you better.

There is something in most reasonable people that tends to let off the hook anyone who apologizes. Our inclination is to say "Oh, Heck, it isn't that bad!" It's a mistake. It doesn't do the job. DP will be back Monday morning with more of the same.

Counter tactic. Acknowledge DP's apology and thank her for it. Then continue with the deliberations as if no apology had been offered. You need to get at the causes of her behavior, why it happened and what you can both do to improve the relationship.

7. *Same facts, different conclusion.*

If you haven't thought through your case against DP you may find that he has turned the tables on you. How? By taking the exact same information and arriving at a different conclusion. And that conclusion is the exact opposite to the one you have presented.

He'll do it because it's easy to do. Easy to do, that is, if you haven't anticipated this kind of a move. When DP finds himself in a tight spot, he does what most people do: He distorts the case so as to favor *his* position rather than yours.

Counter tactic. Have you done the job of preparation? More than that, have you rehearsed? That's the real payoff. When you rehearse, you anticipate roadblocks, and you're ready for the rival explanations and the excuses. Never go into a confrontation cold. You won't be ready. DP will be.

8. *"You'll pay."*

You're about to be blackmailed. DP is about to go into his "I'll take care of you" routine. Since you dare to confront him and suggest that he is imperfect, stand by for retaliation—routine or massive. After all, who do you think you're talking to, an ordinary person?

The standard list of threats. Expect:

- To lose your job, be demoted, transferred, or isolated.
- To lose favor with DP. Implication: Don't expect anything good from me from this point on.
- DP to tell others how bad you are. Naturally, they'll get on your anti-bandwagon.
- That you'll get a reputation as a negative person, a faultfinder.

Counter tactic. Never allow yourself to be blackmailed. It's used too frequently. To bow to it would render all of us ineffective wimps, never daring to challenge anyone.

Listen to the threat. Talk about it. Again, let DP know you are on to her game. Then follow my standard advice: Continue.

9. *Nobody else has complained.*

If nobody else has a problem with me there must be something wrong with you, not me. DPs love this line. They love it because, on the surface, it sounds compelling. It isn't; so don't fall for it.

Actually what DP is trying to do is to play the psychological isolation game. Without anyone on your side you have great problems determining whether or not you make sense. In a society in which we are supposed to respond principally to a majority, you don't have much going for you. You've an N of 1. Statistically, it's hard to generalize from such a small sample.

Counter tactic. Don't buy DP's story. What you need to impress on her is that others may not have had the same problems with her. Or that they may not have the courage to say anything about it. You do.

Secondly, whether or not anyone else has complained is irrelevant. If it's a problem with you, that is sufficient. It is not your job to poll the others. They can fight for themselves.

10. *Silence.*

It doesn't take long to discover the power of silence. When you refuse to talk about something most people don't know how to cope. Negotiation is based on a mutual give-and-take.

DP has learned his lesson well. He knows it's powerful. Now he's using the tactic on you.

Counter tactic. By far, this is the toughest game to fight. There just isn't much good advice available. Here's mine.

Let DP know you are on to the game. Beyond that, you have one hope. Refuse to give up. Your only option is to return again and again. Ultimately, as in some previous examples, DP is going to have to surrender and begin acting like a rational person again.

10
DPs: Exactly How Do I Fight Back?

Though we all love to be evaluated on our individual merits, most people respond to us as a categorical person. We do the same. People obviously display an infinite number of characteristics. Yet is is amazing how they fall into a very few basic categories. So it is with DPs. We may think there are hundreds of varieties. In fact, there are only a few—approximately twelve. This, again, is what my sample revealed time after time. When someone suggests another variety, I find it rather easy to subsume that new type under one of the twelve about to be described.

1. *The unfair (UF)*. By far the number 1 category. More people than ever before feel that they are being treated unfairly by more and more people. They point to preferential treatment accorded some at their expense, others being unfairly promoted over them, getting less merit pay than they think they are entitled to. This only begins the list of grievances. They told me that everywhere you look you see treatment that by any reasonable person's standard is less than fair. Some direct quotes:

- "He has his favorites. If you're not one, you're dead in this company."
- "If you have a Harvard MBA everything's fine. Otherwise you're treated like dirt."
- "If you fawn all over her you'll get everything. If you just do your job she'll hate you."
- "He never honestly evaluates anyone's work. He's strictly political. If you're his buddy, you get all the marbles. If you're not, you get what's left—and that usually isn't very much"!

They also made this interesting observation: That if the other person is fair, then you can excuse just about any of her other negative characteristics. Fairness, they say, is the big criterion.

How UFs Behave

Two men have the same credentials, came to the organization at the same time. Educational background and age are roughly the same. In fact, in virtually every major respect, there is little to differentiate them. Yet one continues to get favored treatment. The other gets what's left. UF can always justify his treatment. Of course it is not favoritism. He can justify it, rationalize it, come up with dozens of excuses—all of which on the surface seem perfectly reasonable. They aren't. It's a case of obviously unfair treatment.

You're promised a lot of things. When the time comes for the payoff, UF finds some reason not to honor the promise. Again, with justifications easy to come by, he floods the floor with them. You have no recourse. At least that's what you think.

Your performance is scrutinized with intensity. Another person's is glossed over. Whatever you do is wrong; what the other person does is just fine. There are two standards operating. One, an impossibly demanding one. That's the one you're struggling under. The other standard is un-demanding. The other person is relaxed, unstressed, complacent. To you, it has the classic look of unfair behavior.

UF likes someone better than she does you. Her favorite gets all the breaks. You get what's left.

Why Are UFs Unfair?

In addition to the reasons common to all DPs (See Chapters 3 and 4) I've found these:

Basic Weaknesses

UF typically succumbs to temptations of all varieties. He sees a more beautiful person—by his standards—and he can't help but give her favored treatment. Others feel they must give their friends the best deal. They don't have the strength to treat them equally.

Still others feel under pressure to give those who scream the loudest the best treatment. Recognize this as the squeaking wheel theory.

Finally, there are the intricacies of politics. UF feels trapped by the complicated network he has developed with other people. In this network are those who are powerful. Then there are the rest. UF is weak inasmuch as he feels he must continually reward those whom he thinks have the real power in the organization.

They Lack Ethical Strength

Ethics is not a word they use often. If they have any, they are situational. That implies that they have a different set of ethics for every situation.

They may know what's right. It's just that they find it too easy not to do it. It is far easier to give into some trumped up excuse or justification.

They See Life as Unfair

UFs tend to feel that you are not entitled to treatment that is any better than what they receive. Why should you get fair treatment when they get unfair treatment? Are you any better than they? Everywhere they look, they say, people are trying to shaft them too. They conclude that the norm of life is to be treated in sleazy, wrong ways. That's what they get. It's also what they hand out.

Blackmail

Who's being blackmailed now? UF is! His friends and co-workers have him over a barrel. They know the kind of person he was and is. Or at least they think they do. At any rate, it's good enough for UF. He now feels that this small band must be given preferential treatment. They get it. You don't. You get least preferred treatment.

Inability to Say No

We're back to the Nice Guy/Gal phenomenon. UF can't say No to anyone. She's tried it. There's just too much anxiety. So she says Yes, or nearly Yes, to the people who push her. You don't push her. You feel that all that is required is that you work hard and you'll be treated well. The pushers come out on top. You barely stay afloat.

They Don't Like You

It's that simple. And it affects how they treat you. They could dislike you and still treat you very well—with fairness. They don't. It's the simplest and most frequently cited reason.

How UF Sees You

Much of this section is discussed in Chapter 4. But to get a complete perspective on UF some of it has to be stated again.

As Weak

UFs tend to kick around the weak, the infirm, the handicapped. They especially kick around those whom they feel will not fight back. You have no personal power in their opinion. So if someone is going to get the unfair treatment you can bet it's going to be you.

As Deserving

UF feels you deserve what you get in life. They reason as follows: If you are so stupid as to let people walk over you, then you should get it good and hard! If you were capable, powerful and a person of strength then people wouldn't dream of treating you the way they do. So don't complain. Turn yourself into someone to be reckoned with.

As an Outgroup Member

You're not a member of UF's in-group. Were you, you wouldn't be treated unfairly. You'd be getting the same good treatment that his buddies are getting. UF reasons that his groupies wouldn't be groupies were they not superior human beings. Since you're not one of them, it follows that you don't have the right stuff. You deserve to get only what's left over.

Fighting It out with UFs

There's nothing very complicated with facing up to the typical UF. You're getting unfair treatment. It must end.

Blow the Whistle on the Unfair Treatment Game

This particular brand of DP is playing the "I'm Unfair" game. Like all games with all DPs you begin by letting her know you are aware of the game. Step 2 is equally standard: You serve notice that you have no intention of playing the game any longer. UF is given no other option.

1. *Your case must be robust and specific.*

A robust case is called for at an even higher level. You need evidence, and plenty of it. And it must be documented. No vague allegations. UF is going to press you for hard core examples. Each one will be dismissed as being a figment of your imagination, paranoia, or your untrusting nature. The remainder will be justified and excused in five different ways.

The solution, again, is to persist. Use all of the procedures discussed earlier, but—above all—don't let him off the hook. You've done that enough already.

2. *Those who use their power in negative ways (NP).*

Everyone has some power. Some have a lot. They have resources, connections. They can do a lot for you, or they can move against you. What we would all like is for people to use the power they have in positive ways—to help us. We'd like better working conditions, more money, more of everything.

Everyone is not quite so cooperative. The DP who uses his power in negative ways does things like this:

- Forces you to do things by veiled or direct threats.
- Demands that things be done her way.
- Lets you know that if you fail to buckle under, you may be out!
- Believes that being the boss gives him the right to dictate how you will do everything—on the job and off.
- Manages by fear. You rarely feel at ease.
- Creates an atmosphere of distrust.

How NP Behaves

It seems like everyone who has power wants to use it. Some like to use it to help people; others to injure or destroy. No one is immune. Everywhere we go we run the risk of coming into contact with someone who is about to unleash some venom, scare us, humiliate us, or force us into some kind of submission, broadly defined.

NP may have real power, money, influence, resources. Or he may have a little. Finally, he may have no real power, but he acts like he does and we tend to believe him. Or we don't know how to fight him.

At the higher level the prototypical NP has you in his employ. His message is abundantly clear: do things my way or suffer the consequences. What might those consequences be? Dismissal, blackballing, bodily injury, blackmail—to name just a few. He makes no secret of it. Take it or leave! If it's a case of sexual harassment, it goes like this: "I hired you, pay your salary. You are a nothing without me. You had better be infinitely grateful. When I want sex you had better be ready."

Lower level bluffs and the little people (who have a little power but not nearly as much as they think) tend to be a little more subtle. The message is the same, but they don't have the guts to spell it out in such bold relief. They imply things a lot more. They leave more to your imagination. They let you wonder just how far they can or will go if you decide not to cooperate.

One of their characteristics is that they don't say things in the presence of witnesses. Nor do they put their threats in writing, for obvious reasons. They tend to be a sneaky lot who lost their sense of ethics long ago, if indeed they ever had any.

They always have been and continue to be one of the major threats in any society.

Worst, they get away with most of their sick behavior.

Why Use Power in Negative Ways?

Nobody knows for sure. They just seem to enjoy telling others what they must do. Of course, there are Freudian interpretations. The trouble is, they don't help us understand NPs very well. Even if we did understand them, would we be prone to excuse them? I hope not!

How NP Sees You

Like all DPs, NP sees you as too weak and gutless to face up to him. Further he is entirely aware of one thing: the fact that you occupy an inferior (in his thinking) position. You're not at his level in the organization, the group, or the relationship. He thinks he really is better and more powerful than you.

Then too you lack the resources to fight such a formidable enemy! If he is your boss, what could you possibly do to fight back? He's holding all the marbles.

In short, NP has little fear of you and is totally convinced that you can and will take it. A little resistance—highly scattered—now and then, but for the most part, you're predictable. You won't fight.

Fighting It Out with NP

You have reasonableness on your side. So push for it. It is unreasonable for anyone to act like NP is acting. That gives you additional power.

Now to that robust case. Accusing someone of using negative power to get her way is serious. I assume you have done your homework several times over. This is going to be a real test.

First, don't be awed by the fact that someone has more rank than you. That's the first thing they are hoping for. You approach NP as you would any other DP. Expect positive results and *look like* you expect them!

Next, present the evidence. It had better be right and thought through. If it is weak and amounts to nothing more than heresay, innuendo, or half truths, you deserve what you get: the wrath of NP. If you have done it right, you will have her with the goods.

Relentlessly press on. Don't gloat that you have her. Be firm, likeable, even when the air is tense and blue.

Last step: sue for peace and make a contract for improved behavior on both your parts. Don't make it an accusation contest. Keep your cool under fire and gently press for better treatment.

NP will admit to nothing. They never do. Since your evidence and case is by necessity based on indirect evidence you have a challenge. By that I mean that you can never actually see negative power. You can only construe it from other's actions. That's why they get away with it so often. It's disguised and hard to pin down.

Consequently, NP may well turn the tables on you. Each instance of alleged negative power will be countermanded with explanations that point to just the opposite. This is the real dilemma in facing up to this particular brand of DP.

Because it is hard to pin down doesn't mean it doesn't exist. Your goal—and it's a tough one—is to show that the evidence clearly points to the use of power in a negative manner.

Since NP won't agree we are once again left only with keeping the monkey on her back. My thoughts on this topic are scattered throughout this book. I repeat them once again: Don't ever take the monkey back. Keep it where it belongs. You may not get immediate results but my experience tells me that if you don't give in, things will improve, often dramatically.

3. *The undemocratic (UD).* Simply stated, most DPs who fall into this category are unconcerned about your rights. Often they are bent on denying them. If the law (or other document) gives you the freedom to offer your opinion, UDs may not. Freedom and rights are not two of their favorite words. To put it briefly, they are quite convinced that they know the right way of doing things—anything. They hardly need your opinion, or input. You might call them "know-it-alls." They know so much that they are entirely convinced that nothing that you could possibly say would be of merit. They are used to having their own way. They are impatient with others whom they view as not as competent, perceptive, or practical. Some of their oft-used phrases:

- "I have very little faith in the average person."
- "I'm perfectly capable of making the best decision myself. Why do I need others wasting my time?"

- "Democracy is inefficient as hell. What we need are people who can make decisions."
- "This isn't a (expletive) democracy. I'm in charge here. I don't need anyone's advice on how to run things. If I do, I'll ask. But don't count on it."

When we are entitled to be included, we resent not being. If we know we have rights and someone doesn't want us to engage in them, we begin to heat up. We all feel we should have input into just about everything. Our opinion may not be informed, but it is still our opinion.

The undemocratic prefer to shut us up and shut us down. They know the range of rights to which we are entitled, but for some strange set of reasons they prefer to circumvent them.

How UD Behaves

One of their favorite tricks is to form cliques and coalitions and leave you out. This often happens in the organization. A, B, and C get together to "run things." You aren't invited. Were this a social organization that would be one thing. It isn't and you're entitled to have your opinion registered as to how things are run.

A second favorite characteristic of the UD is to seek everyone's opinion but yours. Typically there is a handful of favorites. You're not one of them. Too bad. For you. In the short and the long runs you find your power eroded. Then you begin to brood over not being consulted. Things disintegrate: your performance, your attitude. It is not a pretty picture.

At the extreme, you may be treated as an outcast, an undesirable. For whatever reasons, you are excluded—totally. The UD rarely talks to you. When he does, it is for seconds, never for minutes. He always has other things to do.

UD is in the business of playing politics in its seamiest sense. Politics often translates into talking to some people and not to others. You are one of the others.

Why Be Undemocratic?

Invariably UD excludes you for reasons of personal gain. It's always part of a power struggle. You are seen as being any of the following: naive, lacking in power, incompetent, backing the wrong people, in the enemy camp. Consequently, you spell trouble and the solution is to keep you at bay. Those with traits opposite to you as—sophisticated, powerful, competent—are the desirables.

How UD Sees You

As not worth talking to.

Fighting It Out with UD

In addition to the principles cited earlier you must appeal to UD's sense of fair play. He has very little to start with. But like all of us he thinks he does. Ask him if he practices fair play and he'll respond with a loud "Of Course." Don't be fooled by that.

When you appeal to his sense of fair play you must dramatize how it is affecting your behavior in the organization and your relationships with him in particular. Now he is not much interested in the quality of your relationship, so don't expect to score points there.

Drive home your point: You must have fair play. Ask him how he sees the things he is doing to you. Take them one at a time. Evaluate them in terms of fair play. That's your message to him!

Equally powerful and closely related to the issue of fair play is that of motivations—his. What are they? He may not know. Few of us does. But it is powerful on your part to ask anyway. What you're trying to do is show UD that he is wrong in excluding you. Unless he is ready to admit to having sleazy motivations, he's going to have to come up with an explanation that will hold up.

UD may hint that you might be consulted more if only . . . if only you acted more responsible, more caring. Don't worry, he'll have a big list of "if onlys." Great. Now is the time to pump him for everything. Having heard it all, you're ready to make a contract for improved behavior on his part, and yours.

Let him know that you will go out of your way to earn his respect, provided it is reasonable. Give him a plan that you'll follow. Then ask him to follow yours.

It should work. If it doesn't, it's back again come Monday morning.

4. *Those bent on doing you in (shafting you) (SH).* You don't have to be a paranoic to feel that someone is after you. Someone probably is. In every organization I found case after case of the shaft syndrome.

People do try to shaft one another. They try to make the other person look bad, get fired, demoted, or generally fall into disfavor. It's one of the few facts of organizational life—perhaps even of life in general—that sooner or later you will come to the realization that someone is out to get you.

Why they are wanting to get you is another story. The motivations seem simple enough—you committed a major error with respect to them. Or you made them look bad, you sold them out, they don't like your attitude, or your personality.

From your point of view it is a different story. Typically, you feel you are undeserving of this kind of treatment. Most people can't even come up with one good reason why this person would want to do them in. It's all part of the mystery of dealing with this kind of DP.

A few ways people do one another in:

- Portray them to others—especially important people—as incompetent, lacking in judgment, common sense, or social graces.
- Start a hate campaign against them. Begin the process of downgrading everything they do.
- Blame them for whatever goes wrong. Give them no credit for anything that goes right.
- Label them as disloyal, as undeserving to be associated with the group.

Note that the SH who is in the business of trying to shaft you typically follows this m.o! She rarely confronts you directly. It's all underground. On the surface she may appear to be a friend, a supporter. Finally, it may be nigh on to impossible to pin anything directly on them. That is, many of them are exceptionally clever in not ever getting caught redhanded.

You're up against two types, as mentioned above. One is trying to do you in without ever leaving any evidence. Such SHs specialize in undercover operations. It's hard to get any direct evidence on them. They succeed simply because it is incredibly easy to sell someone out. There is a surplus of available methods.

The other type leaves a trail. There's nothing left to your imagination. She is bent on getting your scalp. This may take the form of getting you fired, demoted, out of favor, disgraced in the eyes of the world—or worse.

Why Shaft You?

You've read some of the reasons in Chapter 3. In general, the reasons seem infinite. The top line is this: You are perceived as undesirable! Further, you deserve the punishment they are determined to inflict upon you.

How SH Sees You

You're seen as someone whom they could live happily without, and the sooner the better. You may have something they want, or feel they are entitled to. It may be a specific position or it may be prestige and power.

In simplest terms, you stand in the way of their happiness, success, or other needs. You are unnecessary. If so, the simplest solution is to rid the environment of you. And if she can't send you out the door at least she can neutralize you or inflict a tone of unhappiness in your life.

Fighting It Out with SH

Do you have him with the goods? Great! Confront him directly. Your case must consist of a well drawn up set of incidents. It must be evident to any thinking person that SH was clearly out to do you in. Take out the weak evidence, the heresay and the "I think." Stick with what is demonstrable fact. Then hit him hard with it.

On the other hand, you may have no direct evidence. It's entirely circumstantial, but you know it to be true. The trend is unmistakable. In this case, you must never accuse SH of any crime. Simply provide all of the evidence, even though it can't be classified as hard evidence. Discuss what appears to be a series of unfortunate circumstances and events. Ask directly if SH is responsible for any of these unfortunate affairs in your current life. *Inquire.* That's the key word.

5. *The sloppy communicator (SL).* Gossip, innuendo and rumor are their calling cards. They feel no obligation to stick to what is known. They have little concern for accuracy in communication. They are a threat to all of us for we know not when they will decide to do a job on us.

Like bakers, they serve up every morning a new batch of morsels. As the day wears on, they distribute their morsels strategically throughout the organization.

- Who is sleeping with whom?
- Assorted romance items—the sleazier the better.
- Who will get what job, who will be promoted, who fired.
- Who has committed the major goofs of the week and who is unhappy with that person.
- Who currently is seeking treatment for alcoholism, drugs, or child abuse.
- And—big and juicy—who is pregnant and unfortunately (of course) unmarried.

Will your number come up? Probably several times in the course of a year. My guess is that it already has. By the way, don't expect preferential treatment. The fact that you are good friends means nothing to this particular brand of DP. Loyalty is not one of their strengths.

Sloppy communicators can and do bring organizations to their knees. If allowed to go unabated they will cause massive deterioration in the human relationships of any organization. Worse they can be the very cause of the organization's demise. They need not, and should not, be tolerated.

How SLs Behave

Whispers, softly spoken sentences, innuendo, gossip, rumor and assorted varieties of sick communication. They specialize in how you measure up in the following situations: sex, drinking, gambling, infidelity, and any kind of negative characteristic they can pin on you. They've always "heard" such-and-such about you. Naturally, they would *never* initiate such awful things themselves. Isn't it, they say, a shame how others do these things to you!

SLs talk to people a lot. They spend a lot of time on the telephone. Information is their weapon. Call it dirt. In a very real sense, they are dirt collectors. Never underestimate how dangerous to your health they are.

Why Engage in Sick Communication?

Throughout history there have been numerous theories to account for their behavior. Again we could look at it from a psychoanalytic point of view, but—again—it doesn't help much.

Some people get their kicks from kicking you. That's the simplest explanation. The Why of it is irrelevant. Like so much of human behavior, we don't understand their behavior; but we do understand the consequences.

How SLs See You

They don't. That's one of their interesting characteristics. The person they talk about the most they tend to avoid. With good reason. After all, unless they are totally stupid they know you must have some idea of what they are up to. And they're right. You always do. So they try to stay out of your way lest you precipitate some kind of showdown.

In general, they feel you are among the weaker members of the organization. They, especially, don't expect you to fight back. And like all sick communicators, they're so sick they don't think you have the vaguest idea that they are the ones heading up the smear campaign directed against you.

Fighting It Out with SL

Your first job is to engage in sufficient detective work to get the goods on SL. SL is really a sub-species of DP who is out to shaft you. They do it with words and with nonverbal communication. Mostly words.

Like the person out to do you in, their mission is to make you look immoral, untrustworthy, illegal or generally unattractive—across the board. Their tongue is the weapon.

Make a definite appointment to discuss "communication" in the organization. This will be enough to create instant panic in SL. For now he realizes that it is no longer a secret. You're on to his game. Remember, nobody wants to be accused of spreading rumors about anyone, even if the rumor turns out to be true. It's a dirty business that is not likely to get any new friends. That, in fact, is their real fear. If you finger them as being a sick communicator you will, they assume, begin a campaign of your own—against them.

Lay out the evidence. It isn't likely to be hard evidence since rarely is anything in writing. You must, therefore, overwhelm SL with what you believe to be true. Here's where the need for guts comes in. First, if you have observed, listened, and analysed you are in good shape. Next, you should note where the evidence always seems to point.

SL will admit nothing. They will play the "I'm so shocked that you would accuse me of such a thing" game to the utmost. Don't be fooled by it. Don't swerve. Tighten the screw.

Among many other things, be sure to let SL know (1) that it must end, and that (2) you will be watching carefully for any further signs. That ought to do it. The shock of your confronting her is usually enough to shut her down forever. In a few cases, it may persist or it may rise again. If so, don't wait. Go back. This time your main thrust will be to bring this to the attention of everyone who is anybody. That, be assured, will end the issue.

6. *The closed minded (CL).* At some time we're all guilty of being closed-minded. That is, if you ask the people we work or live with. But there have to be degrees. I'm talking now about that habitually close-minded individual, the one who makes a religion out of not considering yours or anyone's idea. Their characteristics:

- Nothing sinks in.
- They "Yes, But" you to death. Whatever your point, they reply with a But ————— .

Not occasionally. Consistently.

- They don't even acknowledge having heard you.
- They have an arsenal of idea-killer phrases such as:
  - We tried that. It didn't work.
  - People won't understand it.
  - People won't buy it.
  - You don't know what you're talking about.
  - When you're my age, you'll understand.

It appears that the closed-minded DP's main characteristic is this: nobody could possibly be as smart as I am and I wish they would stop trying to advise me!

How They Behave

It's going to be a tough fight. Your patience will be taxed to the uttermost. The CL, by definition, isn't likely to pay an awful lot of attention to you. Above all, then, your job will be to persist and use creative strategies.

CLs treat you like a rock, a nothing. They are adept at not listening. Their nonverbals include not looking you in the eye, of giving the appearance of being in a hurry, and of looking at you like you were insolent.

Why Be Closed Minded?

It's fun, I guess. The ego is entirely gratified when one knows everything! CL has been conditioned along these lines. No doubt having been born with a high IQ, she quickly realized that she stood head and shoulders above the rest of the population. At least, the majority of them. Being thusly convinced, the obvious conclusion was that there was little to be gained by entertaining the ideas of inferior intellects. That's their story.

How CL Sees You

As dumb. At best, hurting in the brains department. You just aren't all that clever. A nice person, sure, but beyond that—nothing!

Fighting It Out with CL

Since CL rarely listens, it's going to grate on you. If you're normal, you'll lose your patience. Don't. Try to remain collected. Nothing positive ever comes from hot-headed action.

You can try to reason, try to present your point of view. It will be ignored. Try again. This time, don't use the same tactic. For instance, if you have been trying to directly penetrate her system, try the indirect method. Let her do the talking until she runs down. Then jump in with your story. If that doesn't work, use your imagination.

This is the toughest nut to crack. Advice in summary: persist and vary your strategy.

7. *The very nice (VN)*. Some people call them super nice. Others call them wimps. Thank goodness they are small in numbers. They deserve the label of DP because they tend to make a mess of operations and relationships. Why? Because they lack old-fashioned courage. They cannot make a decision because you may not like it, or someone else may not. The result is that they try to "nice" their way out of it. They smile all the time. Whatever they tell you is told in what they think is a beautiful way. Since they are so confounded nice, they tell themselves, you'll like everything about them. That's their big need. To be liked by everyone, all of the time.

It doesn't work. One has to have more going for him in life than simply being nice.

Some examples of how the nice person creates big problems:

The very nice boss. Whatever you believe, he believes. He agrees with everything you say. You expect action, but you get none. So you ask why? This DP is clearly in a corner and can't reason his way out. So more being overly nice. To make matters worse, a colleague comes in and says just the opposite of what you have said. The boss agrees with her too. Since he has agreed with both of you, he now finds himself once again trapped. How to get out? Lay more nothing phrases, more handshakes, more smiles. Now there are *two* unhappy people. Make that three. VN can't be very happy either.

Refusing to confront. Much of life demands that we face up to the fact that something must be done. Someone must be rated for merit or promotion. Someone must win something while the other loses. The very nice DP can't bring himself to confront anything important in life. They develop endless ways of getting out of situations without registering a vote, or expressing a preference. We can't count on them to be counted. They, by default, leave it to someone else. The very nice person lacks guts. He wants approval—yours and mine—all of the time.

How They Behave

Very nicely. Cordially, politely—to an extreme. They wouldn't think of making a decision or of saying anything that might embarrass or offend. In a tough decision they just have to suspend judgment or vote "pass."

Why Are They So Very Nice?

Operant conditioning, like all DPs. The processes of reinforcement left them spineless. We have to assume that in their younger days events conspired to turn them into weak excuses for human beings. Were they the playground sissies? I'd say so. Here they are, years later, and they're still sissies. They may not want to be. They may prefer to be people of strength. But more than likely they think it's too late.

51

How VN Sees You

As someone to defer to, to please. She fears that by accident she may insult you, anger you. That is to be avoided.

VN stands in awe of the world in general. They are happy only to the extent you approve of them, or love them. Since these are unlikely states, VNs tend to worry a lot. Each day they brace themselves. What can they do to remain firmly in your good graces? The quest, like the beat, goes on!

Fighting It Out with VN

Be kind, gentle. Then apply firmness. Ask for answers, for decisions, for opinions. You won't get them immediately. Give him a break. With a little strategically placed force, VN will cooperate. They always do.

The best favor you can do for VN is to let him know that you will continue to expect greater definiteness. His age of indecision, in other words, is over. That is the notice you serve.

8. *The prejudiced (PR)*. The prejudiced DP goes after us because of our race, religion, age— or whatever else is bothering him about us. He's the oldest kind of DP known to humanity. Most of us feel that a little bit of prejudice is directed toward us every day. Then there are days when it is thick and obvious.

PRs have no intention of judging us on our individual merits. We fall into a category and their feelings toward people in this category are all negative. Most of the time it's the result of something they picked up in childhood. Racial prejudice is the best example. But it can be picked up anywhere; and it's widespread.

Those most likely to feel the sting of the PRs:

- Older people.
- People with lower IQs.
- Those with learning disabilities.
- The ugly, or otherwise unattractive.
- The rich, famous, beautiful.
- Fat people.
- Races: Asians, Chicanos, Jews, Arabs, Japanese.

How They Behave

PRs are another breed to come at you on two levels: the one you can see and the one you can't. Their philosophy of action is do whatever is necessary to deny you your rights whether that right be to work, be promoted, to a good reputation, to more money, or admission to a group.

Why Be Prejudiced?

Nothing has received more treatment in the mass media. Nobody has the real answer yet. Our best guess at this time is that some of the people who influenced them did so in the wrong way. They were taught prejudice. Seems like a good explanation. How else could they have become that way? Certainly nature isn't prejudiced. Whatever the reasons, they feel compelled to embrace their ideas about other nationalities and religions and sexes, even in the face of overwhelming evidence to the contrary.

How PR Sees You

As inferior. Not only do you not have the *right* stuff, you don't have any stuff at all! You are inherently dumb, incompetent, immoral, lacking in the qualities that make for a human being. You may be entitled to live, but preferably not here.

Fighting Back

With prejudice on all sides of us we have to be careful not to dispel our energies on every little incident. Concentrate on the big, the important cases.

Take age discrimination. It's rampant. No matter how young you are, there's always someone around who thinks you are too old. What's the best medicine for these people?

Ask them, point blank, "Are you an ageist?" That ought to get conversation rolling. They'll answer No, of course. Take it from there. If they aren't, then why do they continually treat you like you really are too old?

Other good leading questions are: "Do you believe in fair play for everyone?" Still another: "Do you stereotype people on the basis of their age?"

For discrimination on the basis of race, religion, or color you can hurl the same questions. Ask them quietly and with dignity. Never behave like the PR.

PRs must know how they are negatively impacting on your life. Now is the time to dramatize. They must visualize exactly what their treatment does to you. Take the time to spell it out. Let them know that your life is worse by virtue of their behavior.

As with all DPs, don't expect PR to own up. But also, in the case of confronting all DPs, a big part of your power comes from letting him know you are very much aware of the sick game he is playing.

Mesh. Exchange perceptions. Contract for better relationships. Then give her a chance to change her tune. If it doesn't change enough, go back. In the final analysis, confronting and changing PR reduces to who can outlast whom!

9. *The verbal overkiller (VO).* The verbal overkiller earns his DP stripes by driving us crazy with words. Too many words. They can't be brief. Every statement must be repeated in yet another way. The examples and illustrations flow with abundance. One line leads to another. Soon we are mentally exhausted just listening to them.

The verbal overkiller attacks our powers of concentration too. With so many words and ideas—most of them redundant—we find our mind wandering. Soon we forget what we came for. By then it doesn't make much difference anyway.

Finally there is the elementary issue of time. Most of us can't afford to get tied up with these people for very long. Yet every encounter with them turns out to be a marathon. They seem unable to appreciate the value of brevity. It just isn't their cup of tea. And we suffer because of it. We need simple answers. We don't get them.

How VOs Behave

The behavioral level is just as described: words—far too many of them. As they continue they fatigue us. We lose our train of thought. We lose our patience. We want to leave, now!

Why Verbally Overkill?

An explanation we can understand goes like this: somebody once told them they were cute and chatty. They took this as a supreme compliment. That's all they needed. From that point on they were convinced that being "outgoing" was the acme of being liked and appreciated. Unfortunately for them—and us—nobody gave them any serious negative feedback. If they did, it was promptly ignored.

How VOs See You

As an empty organism. They perform with you in their presence. It is unlikely that they consider you a normal human being with blood running through your arteries and veins. For the most part, they don't think of you at all.

VOs talk to themselves. They're oblivious to any kind of immediate feedback. And certainly they know nothing about interpreting nonverbals.

If pushed about how they see you they would probably say that you were a nice guy/gal. That's because they never hear you. So by default, you must be an OK person!

Fighting Back

Beyond what has been said in general, there are three strategies: First, upon seeing them, start talking immediately. Demand their attention. Secondly, tell them how they are impacting on you. You must be quick lest they take the initiative from you. Finally, you must talk along with them if they refuse to stop. That's right. Don't let it embarrass you. And don't stop. You will find that they will be the first to stop. Is this bad manners? Of course. Good manners just haven't done the job so far.

On other occasions, gently let VOs know that you intend to have a dialogue. Continue this time after time and you have turned them around. Then watch them. It's easy for them to fall back into their verbal rut.

10. *The one-way communicator (OC).* On the surface you may think the verbal overkiller and the one-way communicator are identical entities. They can be but typically they are not. One-way communicators do all of the talking, all of the time. Your presence is barely recognized. If you attempt to compete with them, they wear you down. They have the amazing ability to keep us from getting a single word in. As with the verbal overkiller, we often leave the scene with an intense feeling of frustration. They're characterized by:

- Unending chatter. There's never a pause.
- A seeming unconcern with the fact that you may also have something to say.
- When you try to talk they invoke one or more of their strategies to silence you: talking faster, talking along with you, talking louder.
- The most they ever give you is a grudging "Yeah" as when you make a comment and they respond "Yeah, well let me tell you more of what I think."
- If by accident you should get the floor, they will interrupt you to regain it. Then they will make no reference to anything you may have said.
- By definition, they are an egocentric group bent on having their own way. If you don't like it, then *you* have a problem. At least, that's what they think.

They're everywhere. They engender the same kind of reaction from everyone: disgust. If we let them, they can ruin our work life, or our life, period!

How OCs Behave

OCs are totally undemocratic about this business of communication. They see no value in whatever comes from your mouth. They do not, like verbal overkillers, tire you with endlessly pursuing the same point. They talk about anything—about lots of things. Their most important behavioral characteristic is this: they are dead set on preventing you from saying a single word if they can possibly help it. Accordingly, any attempt on your part to express an opinion or make any kind of statement will meet with instant and massive retaliation.

Why Be a One-Way Communicator?

Like the close minded, OC doesn't feel that you have much going for you. To them you are an average mentality, at best. Those whom they consider super brilliant—and there are very few—they let talk.

Do you get the feeling OCs have an inflated opinion of their talents? Right! They do. You see, nobody of power has challenged them before. The result is they continue to enjoy it.

How OCs See You

Your input is not wanted, so accept it and remain silent! If they thought you had an idea that was worth anything, they'd ask you for it. So far they haven't asked you. So don't volunteer!

Fighting Back

Specifics: As with VO the first thing you must do is to grab the initiative right off the bat. Start talking and don't stop until you have made your points.

Give OC your oration on democracy in communication, the fact that we should all have our moment to say what we too think.

Next, ask OC for motivations. This will be totally embarrassing, but press on anyway. When you ask him why he performs this way you sensitize him in two ways: (1) He is forced to come to grips with the idea that someone doesn't appreciate his behavior, and (2) He is likely to give it serious thought.

Finally, you provide a little bit of elementary instruction in the act of two-way communication. Your message to him is that we both have to listen some, talk some, and switch from one mode to the other. They may resent your preaching to them but sometimes that's exactly what it takes to wake them up.

Then sit back and wait. Chances are excellent he will begin to turn around. If not, re-cycle the whole process.

11. *The Pseudo Helpless (PH)*. It's nice to know there's someone around when you need a helping hand. It's hard to know everything we need to know to survive. We ask for assistance and usually get it. The model goes something like this: I've done all I can, but I still seem unable to understand. Would you help me? Under those conditions, virtually any one of us says Why Not!

Now to the other side of the coin. You're asked for help when the solution is staring them in the face. Or you are told "I don't know anything about computers." You tell them to turn on the switch and start learning.

The line is repeated: "But I told you I don't know anything about them." Clearly the pseudo helpless game is being played. They want *you* to do it. They want you to spend hours showing them when they could learn it easily on their own by consulting the manual. It's strictly a case of infantile perseveration. As kids we all said occasionally, "I don't know how to," hoping the adult would jump in and do it. Too often one did. Most of us got over playing the helpless game. A few are still holding out.

How the PHs Behave

In a way that irritates. They never have the tools. Nor do they have the skills. They wouldn't know where to begin, or end. They don't understand. It's all so confusing. We're expecting too much from them—they say!

Why Play the Pseudo Helpless Game?

PHs behave that way because we too long let them get by with it. Now it is a central part of their repertoire of behaviors. It has worked and continues to work. They lack initiative. They prefer not to work or otherwise put themselves out. Better that you do it for them. They are overprotected brats, pushing their luck to the limit.

How PHs See You

As a pushover. They know exactly who will play their game and who will not. They've determined that you will. In their eyes, you are either weak, lack the courage to tell them No, or you are playing the game of super nice guy/gal.

Fighting It out with PH

The advice is brief and effective: Don't give in. Provide reasonable help and assistance. Then turn them loose. Set deadlines and quotas. Let them know the consequences of their behavior. Then back up your words. Above all, don't get angry and do it yourself.

12. *The Insensitive (IN).* Consideration, sensitivity to others, just plain good manners— these are the things that make human interaction tolerable. When we forget them—or neglect them—we can sense the difference it makes. People get offended. They get upset with us. So most of us go out of our way to be decent, to treat others in a way that suggests we respect, like, and approve of them. Most of us. Not all of us. It's a minority, but a powerful minority of DPs who have the questionable distinction of having very bad manners. You don't have to look far to see one. They are very obvious. Every organization has at least one. Statistically, they account for one of the largest categories of DPs.

How They Behave

Operationally defined, the IN variety of DP goes through these kinds of motions:

They interrupt. Their thoughts and contributions are much more important than are yours. So they must be heard! If you happen to be talking, the message to you is clear: Shut up! They engage their mouths (certainly not their brains) and cut you off at the pass. You are left with your mouth hanging open as they unload their tons of words. No matter who's in the middle of a sentence they can't resist taking over. They call it being "vigorous and actively involved." It's nothing of the sort. It's rude!

They publicly embarrass. INs like a crowd—two, three, or hundreds. It gives them an opportunity to belittle you but good. The bystanders make it more exciting for them. It's an audience, and INs love an audience. It increases the embarrassment factor. And, too, they have the misguided impression that the bystander always sides with them. Too bad they never bother to check that assumption. They'd find out it isn't true.

They love crowds for another reason: They are afraid to tell you things one-on-one. That takes guts, something they are short on. So they wait for others to appear on the scene.

They don't use your name. Civilized people who are expected to know and remember your name do just that. Our name is important to each of us. And one way of recognizing a person's individuality is to use it. If you've been working in an organization for five years, then the people you work with ought to know your name. Let's say there is a departmental meeting. You make a comment. Then someone prefaces her remark by saying "Well, I agree with *him*. . . ." Why *him*? Doesn't she know your name? If she doesn't, there must be something wrong with her mentality. Maybe not. It may just be part of a defective way she has of relating to people. In fact it may just be one of the crude ways of treating people she has developed over the years. In effect, she has grown insensitive.

They ignore you. When we ignore someone we suggest they are unnecessary—that we and the world could get along without them quite nicely. If we ignore their comments or point of view it amounts to the same thing. INs ignore you in a variety of ways. When you make a comment, they:

- Change the subject.
- Say "Yeah" or mutter something equally meaningless. Then they proceed with *their* brilliant analysis of the situation—which is totally unrelated to yours.
- Say nothing. Just look at you as if you were the dumbest thing on earth.
- Never deal with what you just said.
- Act as if you haven't said anything.
- Give out with nonverbals that let you know they think you would be better off staying at home—or whatever.

They say "humorous" things about you—and some people believe them. You tell the person next to you that you were hospitalized for a day. Out of nowhere pops IN and lets loose with "But you did survive the abortion—that's something!" INs, insensitive by nature, thinks that's funny. No one else does, least of all you.

Some of their other indelicate nonsense includes:

- Laying some offensive nickname, or label, on you: hot lips, bubbles, or The Scourge of the Second Floor.
- Using you as a tasteless illustration. "You should be more like Smith here—completely dishonest!" (Laughter)?

The list is endless. The reaction of the person on the receiving end is predictable: they would enjoy publicly flogging IN, and often seem on the verge of doing just that.

They insult your intelligence. It's done in a variety of ways. They spend a lot of time informing you of things you already know. If you make an intelligent observation, they wonder, aloud, how someone with your limited capabilities could possibly come up with something that brilliant. They especially like teaching and instructing. To them, your mind is a blank slate. There is no way possible that you could understand the situation in the Far East, the ins and outs of the stock market, or how a bill goes through Congress. So they will take time out of their busy schedule to inform you. You're the student and they are the master teacher. Since you know nothing you can only listen. Should you venture a comment you can bet it will be ignored.

They treat you as an object rather than as a human being. This effectively summarizes the IN personality. It seems that they have this awful blind spot in their personalities. Normal manners is not one of their concerns. It is their primary deficit.

Why Such Inconsideration?

In addition to the reasons given for difficult people behaving the way they do (Chapter 3), are there any specific reasons for someone playing the IN role? My interviews didn't get much more than I've already discussed. Just a few more glimmers. From INs themselves:

- "That's just the way I am. It's me."
- "Everyone has an interpersonal style. I have mine; you have yours. Who's to say which is better?"
- "You get nowhere being a nice guy."
- "It takes too long to molly-coddle people. I don't have that kind of time."
- "People have no problem understanding me. They know where I stand."
- "I'm not in this group (relationship) to be liked, necessarily. I'm in it to get things done."
- "If people don't like my style, then *they* have a problem. *I* don't."
- "When you're nice to people they invariably take advantage of you."

That's what they told me! Here's what I told them:

Nobody buys "It's just the way I am" anymore. In fact, they never did. It's far too convenient. Furthermore, it's untrue. It's nothing more than a sick excuse for behaving like a child!

Who's to say which style is better? Everybody. Where do they line up? The overwhelming percentage on the side of reasonable good manners. People don't demand excessive politeness. They just want you to extend ordinary courtesies. It's what makes us want to go to work.

You get nowhere being a nice guy? False. You get everywhere. People will like you; and if people dislike you, you're not going to go very far.

Does it take too much time to be nice to people? Not to my knowledge. In fact, most people find that treating people sensitively makes it easier and faster to conduct all kinds of business.

"People have no problem understanding me." True. And what they understand they don't like. They would also understand acceptable manners. Don't equate boorish treatment of people with openness and directness. There is no necessary connection.

To the statement "I'm not here to be liked; I'm here to get things done" I say this: You'll get an awful lot more done if you don't turn people off. In addition, I think you *are* here to be liked. We all are. Nothing good comes from engaging in unlikeable behavior.

How about the argument "*You* have a problem. *I* don't." Response: I've heard that line thousands of times. The variations are numerous. They contain a major flaw in the IN's thinking. It goes like this: The world is wrong; I'm right. The world must adjust to me because I know I'm the one who's really in step with the universe.

Finally we have the last resort of IN—"nice people get taken advantage of." It's something his father whispered to him during his little league days. It really sank in. He believes it. The fact is he has never tried being nice to people, so he has no idea how gratifying it can be.

How IN Sees Us

IN, being a sub-species of DP, has all of the characteristics of DPs discussed in Chapter 4. What more can I say about them? Very little. Their methods of operation are easy to spot. Still I've noticed a few additional modes of behavior that can help us understand and cope more effectively with them.

With respect to how INs see us my evidence leads me to conclude that:

- They seem unable to pick up on normal non-verbal communication. The signs that their behavior is being unappreciated, or totally rejected, does not register with them. Call them thick-headed, dense, socially insensitive—whatever. They just don't have the capability to recognize what people are telling them with their body language. Everyone present can see it. They can't.
- There is some evidence that they think the rest of the world envies them for what they call their "straightforward" (vulgar) treatment of people. And, further, they are quite convinced that we'd all love to be like them. It's just that we don't have the guts.
- They think their sense of humor is 100% American, nothing short of superb! They wonder why the rest of us are so serious and lacking in lightheartedness.
- They tend to think that you don't think much about what they are saying. In other words, no matter how rude they get you will let it enter Ear #1 and allow it to freely flow out of Ear #2. This phenomenon has been called the fallacy of the empty organism.
- It rarely occurs to them that you consider them to be: stupid, out of it, a social jerk or misfit, a clown, an imbecile, or a detriment to progress.
- They can't understand why you would be offended by their behavior. Often they are shocked—they stand in disbelief—if you decide to fight back. They ponder the situation and wonder what could have possibly gotten into you. "You sure are defensive today"!
- Finally, as with many DPs, they tend to think that because no one tries to stop them, that they must approve of their behavior. In this respect, let me add that INs tend to misinterpret the feedback that is sent out. Unquestionably, they suffer from misconstruction of social reality.

Fighting It Out with the INs.

1. *Confrontation.* This is the one approach common to all DPs. They must be directly confronted. Your job is to exchange perceptions. You begin with a kind of summary appraisal of the situation which says, in effect, this is how I see the problem, how I see myself, how I see you, how I feel, and how I see it affecting both our lives. You then ask for responses—her perceptions and feelings.

Be specific. Give important and high impact examples. You can do this because you've done your homework. Yours is not a reaction to an isolated instance. It's a highly visible, recurring situation. Drive that point home—unceasingly!

Remember, confrontation is for your mutual benefits. It's not a weapon for your exclusive use. By its very nature it gives you both an equal opportunity to explore the conflict. This means you're obligated to talk *and* listen.

2. *Demonstrate how the behavior affects you.* DPs, we know, are hard to get through to. Often, simple explanations have little impact. That's when it's time to dramatize. Use analogies, narrative, quotations, statistics, extended examples—anything that will arrest attention.

Part of your demonstration should include a terse analysis of where their insensitive behavior is leading. Project the consequences in detail. You are saying this: "Shape up or face the consequences—and you won't like those consequences!" How you say this is a reflection of your personal style. I emphasize only that it must be said.

3. *Ask for reasons and motivations.* You won't get the real reasons, but try anyway. People often do not understand their own behavior. So they can't very well tell you. Beyond that, their motivations may be socially unacceptable. To admit to them would be tantamount to admitting to being emotionally sick. So what good does it do to ask for motivations? This. You force IN to examine his motives, to take a good look inward. It could result in his being shocked by his own behavior. There's another reason. It's good for IN to think that you are evaluating his mental and emotional health. It's going to make him re-appraise his behavior toward you. Finally, when you ask for motivations, IN has got to say something. If he admits he has been mistreating you then there must be a reason. That's where you've got him. There has never been a valid reason for behaving toward another in an outlandish way.

4. *Serve notice that you expect improved treatment.* Back to one of my giant principles: It's amazing what you can get by just asking. It'll work here too. The object is to openly ask IN to change her unacceptable behavior—and to do it now. There's nothing to think over. You spell it out so that there is no chance for misunderstanding your position. Don't be equivocal. The time is now—not tomorrow, or even two hours from now.

You must also, in a quietly assertive manner, inform IN that, effective as of this moment, you will react to any breach of reasonably good manners immediately. Your desire is not to embarrass, but if embarrassment enters, then so be it. He'll just have to live with it. This is another way of letting it be known that you have no intention of being kicked around any longer. It's over!

5. *Press for a contract for improved behavior on her part—and on yours.* There's nothing more powerful than entering into a contract in which both parties know the rules. Why be satisfied with a "gentleman's agreement." You'll win more by stipulating the exact behavior you wanted changed. That has impact! Then there's you. By now, your confrontation should have given you a lot to think about. IN no doubt has laid some "defects" on you. The contract, then, has got to include a change in some of your irritating, or otherwise unacceptable, behaviors. Fine. Let it. Put it in the contract. What you end up doing, in other words, is admitting that at least some of IN's behavior is a reaction to your behavior. If you do this, you'll have a workable contract. Otherwise, words, cheap, cheap words!

11
What to Say When DPs Leave You Speechless

"But what exactly do I say?" People want to know. "DP comes roaring back and there I sit. Now what do I do? Give me some words." All right I will. But remember, these are prototypical, generic responses. The exact words you use will depend on your personal communication style. They are responses that can be used repeatedly with positive effect. Study them and make them a natural part of your response repertoire in dealing with DPs.

The Model

When DP does anything to sidetrack you, to get you off both her case and her back—fight back. First, let her know that you are aware of the sub-game being played. Then let her know you are serious and intend to continue. Ask for cooperation and—especially—for better treatment. Remember: Never give in! Keep that monkey on DP.

In the illustrations that follow watch how the model is employed unceasingly. In all cases *DP* will stand for the particular *DP* in question, *YOU*—naturally—means what it says, and *ID*, illustrative dialogue.

ID #1: Profanity

DP: "Listen you dumb _____ . I don't need some stupid _____ like you coming in here with a story like that! Who the _____ do you think you are!"

YOU: "Joe, I hear the obscenities. Frankly, we don't need them. And I don't appreciate your talking to me in that kind of language. So I'm asking you to dispense with it and talk to me as a reasonable human being. We have a serious problem and I know we both want to get it resolved."

OR

YOU: "Mr. Smith, I treat everyone with respect and dignity. And I expect similar treatment from them. So—please—dispense with the foul language so that we can turn this into a fruitful discussion. We have a serious situation in need of improvement. Shall we get on with it?"

ID #2: "See me later—much later."

DP: "Hey, gotta go! See you next week some time."

YOU: "Fine. Can we discuss when it would be mutually convenient." I'm available on Tuesday and Thursdays, all morning. Want to check your calendar? By the way, we have a lot to discuss. So let's make it for an hour."

OR

YOU: "We're all busy, Jane. I know that. But this is the second time you've had to suddenly leave. I'm sure it's important. But the problem we have is important too. Now, I can come back next week—and the week after. And, if necessary, I will. Of course, it's to our mutual benefit to work out a solution to this problem."

ID #3: "You can't believe how sorry I am."

DP: "Beth, I just wasn't thinking all these weeks. I guess I've hurt you—and I'm very, very sorry."

YOU: "I accept your apology, of course. But we've got to get to the bottom of what happened, and why. I think it's complicated and we'll both have to do our best to sort it all out. And I know you want to, just as I do."

OR

YOU: "I know you say you're sorry, Miss Bartlett, and I have no reason to question your sincerity. This is, of course, the third time it has happened. So we've got to work out a solution. I want that. And I'm sure you do."

ID #4: Verbal overkill

THE SCENE: For the past 5 minutes, DP has been literally ranting. He's made the same point seven times.

YOU: (Interrupting and talking along with him. He finally stops.) "I'm sorry to be rude, Bob, but I'm out of alternatives. We have a lot to talk about and we seem to be making little headway. I'm sure you, like me, want to work toward a better relationship. Now, if I may I'd like to propose that we . . ."

OR

YOU: "Bob!" (Loud enough to shock him into stopping.) "I'm sorry, but we've just got to make better use of our time. We simply can't get bogged down with long speeches. You can't. I can't. So let's establish a ground rule: brief responses."

ID #5: The One-Way Communicator

THE SCENE: As in ID #4, DP is relentless with her outpouring of words. You have the distinct feeling you are being treated like a non-person.

YOU: "Susan, please listen to me." (Spoken with appropriate loudness—almost a shout. The body language, while positive, leaves no doubt but that you are going to be heard, or you'll know the reason why.) Susan pauses. You continue. "You have lots of important things to say, I know. I do too. So we're both going to have to be democratic about this: So let's adopt a rule: We'll talk some, listen, then talk some more. We'll respect the fact that each of us has a lot to say. Otherwise we'll get nowhere. I know you don't want that. Neither do I. We have a real problem here and it's going to require our best efforts."

OR

YOU: "I'm sorry I have to resort to what might appear to be rudeness, Susan, but I—as well as you—have a lot to say. I simply must have an equal opportunity. I know you believe in fair play. I do too. I want you to tell me whatever you have on your mind. But I'll need my turn too. So please cooperate so that we can tackle this problem we have and get it resolved."

ID #6: "I'm innocent."

DP: "I hear what you're saying, Julie. But I hope you don't think I had anything to do with this—because I didn't. End of conversation."

YOU: "I know you feel you had no part in this, Mr. Jenkins, but I can assure you I've done my homework. If we can continue, I'm sure you'll understand why I approached you rather than Johnson. I'm not accusing you of anything, of course. But I'd like an opportunity to share my perceptions of how I see things. I hope you'll give me yours too."

OR

YOU: "I'm sure you'd like to end the conversation. But I'm afraid I can't oblige. You see, Mr. Covell, there is no question in my mind that I'm talking to the right person. If I find that I'm mistaken, I'll apologize. But right now I think it's crucial that we continue to discuss this."

ID #7: "I want to talk to a man."

THE SCENE: DP is demanding that a product be shipped within three days. You (female) have explained why this cannot be done. His next statement:

DP: "Let me talk to a man."

YOU: "Sir, I am the director of inside sales. Nothing would be accomplished by talking to a male member of our staff. He will only have to confer with me once again. I'm very willing to help in any way that I can. You're a valued customer. I hope you realize—on the other hand—that there is a distinct division of responsibility in our organization and for the benefit of our customers we follow it to a T."

OR

YOU: "Sir, that statement sounds slightly anti-female. I'll forgive you, of course. I know you didn't intend to give the impression that I was incompetent. Now, then, is there something else I can do for you?"

ID #8: "Don't you like it here?"

THE SCENE: The conversation thus far involves one major issue: DP's apparent repeated discrimination of you on what appears to be your age. In the middle of one of your lines DP interrupts you:

DP: "What's the matter, don't you like it here."

YOU: "Mrs. Simon, I like many things about my job. That really isn't the topic at the moment. Now what I seem to be getting from you is a veiled—if not an obvious—threat. Now, I'm sure you didn't mean it to sound like a threat. So I'd be happy to forget it and proceed because we'll need all the time we can get if we're going to get started at resolving the problems existing between us."

OR

YOU: "As a matter of fact I like it here very much. We do seem to have some problems that I think we'd both profit from discussing. And, Mrs. Wickford, I really would appreciate if you would refrain from issuing threats. I'm sure we can discuss our differences as two reasonable individuals. Now then . . ."

ID #9: "What a stupid remark!"

THE SCENE: The professor asked for opinions. You gave yours. This elicited from the professor:

DP: "That's the stupidest remark I've heard in years." You later stop by his office.

YOU: "Dr. Forley, I'm asking that you refrain from hostile outbursts directed at me. You embarrassed me and made me an object of ridicule among my classmates. Since I pay for taking classes I assume I am entitled to courteous, humane treatment. Please respect my position as a student as I do yours as a professor. Now, if you have a moment I'd like to discuss next week's assignment."

OR

Immediately following the remark, while still in class:

YOU: "Dr. Forley, I do not appreciate being reduced to an absurdity. In the future I shall expect treatment that is commensurate with your position as instructor and mine as a student in good standing at this university."

ID #10: The silent treatment.

THE SCENE: One of this DP's weapons is to refuse to talk about anything unpleasant or controversial. You hit a nerve, then she goes into her silence act.

YOU: "Debbie, I realize it isn't pleasant for either of us to discuss this. But we have a real problem that won't go away on it's own. I just can't walk out that door because you don't want to talk. I'm just going to have to stay here until you change your mind. If we both cooperate we can work out an acceptable solution."

OR

YOU: "You can sit there in silence, Debbie, but what will that accomplish in the long run? Nothing! I'll just be back again and again until we get this thing resolved. So I'd really appreciate it if you'd make the effort to continue the discussion."

ID #11: The Idea Killer

THE SCENE: This DP plays the role of the negativist for all it's worth. One day, in his presence, you suggest a new method of evaluating employees. His response:

DP: "That won't work. We tried it years ago."

YOU: "I certainly respect your experience, Al, but the world of management has changed over the past 25 years. I think the idea has some merit. At least, give me a chance to outline it. Then you can give your reaction."

OR

YOU: "I know you're a positive person, Al, but that response sounds awfully negative. I'd really appreciate it if you'd delay your response until I can tell you the whole story."

ID #12: Sloppy Listening

THE SCENE: You and DP are discussing a point. DP seizes upon something you said and obviously distorts your position, in the process making you look absurd.

YOU: "Mr. Pratt, I would very much appreciate it if you would make the effort to understand what I'm saying. You seem bent on distorting everything I say. I'll do my best to try to understand you too. That's fair play, and I know you believe in fairness. Now, how about giving me your response to . . ."

OR

Slowly and painstakingly you re-explain your point. Then you say to DP:

YOU: "Now, Mr. Pratt, that's what I was trying to explain. But you cut me off before I could complete it. So, please allow me to make my point before criticizing it. If we pay close attention to one another we'll resolve our problem much sooner."

ID #13: A response to hostile humor

THE SCENE: In the presence of several of your co-workers, DP has emitted one of her favorite hostile/humorous (to her) one liners.

YOU: "Jane, I'll tell you straight away, I don't appreciate hostile humor. I feel it's degrading. It simply cannot be tolerated. Consequently, I'm asking that you talk to me in more positive ways."

OR

YOU: "Jane, I realize you don't think there is anything wrong with hostile humor. Most people don't react when you use it on them. That, of course, is their choice. I personally find it offensive and would prefer that you use a more positive brand of humor where I am concerned."

ID #14: Why don't I cry?

THE SCENE: DP uses crying as a weapon. On this occasion, just as you seem to be reaching the important point in the conversation she does it again:

YOU: "Mrs. Cantor, I find it difficult to negotiate with someone who is crying. Why don't you take a few moments to get yourself together, then we'll continue." (DP normally regains her composure in a minute or two.) "Great. Now, let me ask you how you perceive me in this instance . . ."

OR

YOU: "Mrs. Cantor, I've found it to be counterproductive to try to carry on an intelligent discussion when one of the parties is crying. So please try to keep your composure. We have an awful lot to discuss.

ID #15: "You intimidate me."

THE SCENE: This DP likes to avoid discussion by laying a guilt trip on you. His speciality is telling you how intimidating you are. This, of course, means that he would be at a disadvantage in any encounter with you. So why bother.

YOU: "Don, I can't tell you that I don't intimidate you. Perhaps I do. It seems in this world that someone is always intimidating to someone. But it's something we just have to accept and live with. So—intimidating or not—we're going to have to sit down and work our way through this problem."

OR

YOU: "Don, in some ways you intimidate me. But I try not to let it bother me. And if there is something in me that intimidates you, I hope you'll try to adjust too. You see neither of us can do an awful lot about how people react to us. We just have to do our best. So, let's give it another try."

ID #16: "But you have it all wrong."

THE SCENE: DP admits that he committed certain acts. What he objects to is the interpretation you've put on those acts.

YOU: "Paula, I'm open to your explanations, of course. I do consider myself an open-minded person. But please let me assure you that I haven't arrived at these conclusions hastily. I've done my homework well. So, please let me demonstrate to you how I came to believe what it is I believe."

OR

YOU: "Differences of opinion, Paula, are what makes for horse racing. We both know that. And certainly I respect your view on these things. However, I have studied these situations carefully. So I would appreciate it if you would listen to my line of reasoning before you conclude I'm wrong. Let's take that first issue. . . ."

Summary

I could present example on top of example. You don't need any more. The model is always the same. Your message to DP? "You're not going to shut me up. I have communicative rights and I intend to take full advantage of them." You are, in effect, calling DP's bluff. And that is what fighting it out with DPs is all about!

12
The Briefly-Encountered DP

They come in the form of customers, clients, information-seekers, to mention a few. They want something. And the thing they want can't be obtained without going through you. You are a clerk, secretary, registrar, office manager, or an assistant to the boss. You are the one on the firing line. They meet you first. Most of the time you can facilitate their getting whatever it is they came for. In other cases you have to make the decision as to whether or not you will allow them to go any further—to see someone else: the boss, another person in the organization, or anyone higher in authority, or expertise, than yourself.

The briefly-encountered DP (BE) is so named because he is from outside the organization. You encounter him. Then he's gone. He may or may not return. In some instances you see him often. In this case he may be a steady customer, or client. Examples:

Secretaries meet these kinds of BEs:

- "I demand to see Mrs. Greene." Your job: screen her request. Mrs. Greene cannot possibly see everyone who wants to see her.
- "I want to discuss this problem with a *man*"! You're female. You begin to do a slow burn.

Inside sales representatives, these kinds:

- "I need this order and I need it now." You know that getting it into production immediately is out of the question.

Retail sales clerks, these kinds:

- "I bought this stereo last week and it sounds terrible." That's just the beginning, of course. Unless you act fast, she'll shout you to your knees.

Finally, anybody who is an information source may be on the receiving end of this kind of request:

- "I have to know, right now, how many of these credits will apply in my case." To get the information would require hours.

The number and combinations of situations in which a BE arrives on the scene are innumerable. For millions of people around the world encounters of this type constitute the bulk of their day. And a very large percentage leave work each day with frayed nerves, knotted stomachs, headaches, and assorted stress symptoms.

It is a tribute to the human race that most people are reasonable, polite, and understanding. What is left is the hard corps of BEs—again the ones who increase the misery in our lives all out of proportion to their numbers.

Get Straight How Much Authority You Have

Virtually everyone works for someone else. We all have a boss, report to someone, have a manager. That boss may be the doctor, dentist, psychiatrist, office manager, head clerk, chair of the department, or assistant vice president.

Have a long talk. Find out exactly how much authority they want to give you in dealing with BEs. Few people bother to discuss this important matter with the boss. They guess a lot, or they learn from years of experience. Neither is recommended. What you need is to go down the list of BE's typically undesirable behaviors and determine how far you will be backed when things come crashing down. Again, without this assurance you risk being left hanging on that creaking limb.

Here's what you'll find: The boss will back you all the way so long as you are optimally assertive, don't do anything that will reflect badly on the organization, and you are *right*. Being right in this case means that a random group of reasonably intelligent people would do the same thing under similar circumstances.

The boss wants you to deal fairly and respectfully with everyone. This means you are expected to engage in likeable behavior, preserve the dignity of the other person, never lose your cool, but never take obvious abuse from anyone. Above all, she expects none of these: curt remarks, hostile humor, bad non-verbals, obscenities, and threats of your own.

The BE: Fighting Back

Expect and be ready. BEs tend to repeat their behaviors. That's why it is easy to categorize them. After you've been through your first dozen you too will recognize the tactics: threats, bullying, demands, stern nonverbals. It follows that if we can predict BE's behavior, we can be ready for them. This means that if the first five leave you at a loss for words, the sixth one you are ready for. The more you can anticipate and practice appropriate responses the most likely you are to remain in control of the encounter.

Stand up. If BE is standing, you stand up too. To remain seated puts her in a superior position, much like a judge in a courtroom. You're being talked down to, with all that implies. It is better to ask BE to be seated, next to you, not in front of you. Avoid having her sit or stand a large distance from you. This creates the impression that you are enemies. It is also more difficult for someone to aggress against you if they are standing or sitting close to you.

Never panic. Keep your cool under fire, no matter what. Commit yourself to that position. Panic behavior is always regretted. It's bad for you and the organization. If necessary, keep some object in your hand to help condition you. After many encounters, you can throw it away. It will become part of your personality.

Keep the nonverbals positive. BEs create stress in us. The result is that we are likely to begin giving the appearance of unhappiness. Don't let it happen. Like panic behavior, it fosters a bad image. Nobody wants to deal with someone who looks like they are ready to consume everything in sight. Worse, it is a sign of an amateur. Professionals learn to stay in the positive mode, regardless—and this includes body language.

In fact, keep everything positive. Positive nonverbals make a statement. So do positive verbals. They're all part of the positive you. BEs may be negative, but don't let it rub off on you. They may be talking tough. Let them.

Ask for better treatment. The best cure for obnoxious treatment is to ask for improved treatment. You will recall this as one of my fundamental principles of human relations. You determine that BE is engaging in unacceptable behavior, and you tell him so—positively. Then you tell him the kind of treatment you want. It works!

Expose threats. Open threats or the veiled variety should be tolerated by no one. BE should be pinned down: "Mr. Smith, that comment sounds like a threat. Did you intend it to be?" Recognize that threats play a big role in BE's repertory of behaviors. Expose them and talk about them. Finally, let her know that it is not your style to entertain threats of any kind.

You can't give in to threats and stay in business. By you, I mean the person on the firing line, the owners, top management, the shareholders, or anyone connected with the organization. As I indicated earlier in another perspective, threats and blackmail continue to flourish worldwide. For those of you sitting at the main entrance to the organization I mean this: BEs from the beginning have and will continue to use threats on you. That's how they get their way—if you let them.

- "If we can't get this shipment by noon tomorrow, we'll have to take our business elsewhere."
- "I'm afraid I'm going to have to talk with Reverend Walden about this. I know he'll understand."
- "You are aware of the fact that the Z Corporation does an awful lot of business with your company, aren't you?"
- "If Dr. Ober were here, I know he would agree to this."
- "I'm afraid you and I are going to have to sit down and have a little chat with Bill."
- "Now I don't want to divulge any information I have about you. But if you push me, I may have to."

All are threats—forms of blackmail. Are you about to weaken and give in? I wouldn't. If you do, it's good-bye to your integrity and your personal power. BE has hit the sensitive nerve ending. From this point on you will be known to BE as an easy mark. A little threat of blackmail and you cave in! Hardly the reputation you want. If you can't negotiate with BE out of principles then both you and your organization will not survive in the long haul. Like all negative communication, the word will go forth. Then everyone will jump on the wagon!

Minimally justify. The problem with justifying your life, your position, your behavior is that it knows of no end. One can always ask one more Why? And BE knows well the power it can have. Once you get into the justification trap you soon find that BE has you. He finally got you into an indefensible position. You have no escape. To extricate yourself, you must now tell him that it is just the way it is, or backtrack and reinterpret your previous comments. Either weakens you and DP is ready to move in for the final thrust.

Minimal justification begins with stating that the organization's policies, rules, and procedures state that "..........". Be brief! If pushed further, you need only state that these procedures are intended for maximum fair play for all concerned, to reflect total honesty, to be sensitive to clients and customers. At this point, justification should end.

Don't allow Yes-But to get started. Since BE loves to trap you into justification, it follows that she likewise loves to play Yes, But. Yes, But is another form of pushing you to justify. BE says Yes. Then he adds the qualifier which always begins with But! When Yes, But begins do not reply. Stick with your game plan. Powerful people refuse to engage in such counter-productive maneuvers.

Tell what you stand for, not what you don't stand for. "We stand for fair play for all." Or "We don't give in to bullies." The first statement is positive all the way. The second invokes negative suggestion. And it makes for defensiveness. Power comes from telling others what it is we stand for. Remember it well. We can always talk about positives or negatives. Getting bogged down in negative assertions lets BE know that you lack confidence.

End the conversation when it's over. BE has learned that he can out-talk you simply by refusing to stop. It is the game of repetition. BE brings up the same points again and again. You don't want to be rude. Yet you run the risk of continuing the conversation for hours. That you cannot afford. Others are waiting, and time—for all of us—is at a premium. What to do?

Summarize your position, restate your organization's policy in streamlined form. Then end— on a highly positive note. Excuse yourself. Rude? Hardly. No one really expects you to fight it out with BE for the rest of the day. A firm stand was called for. You took it.

What About BEs Rights?

BE has the same rights we all have. She has a right to expect fair treatment, sensitivity, and positiveness. Beyond that, she has no claim on you. Do everything you can to be helpful. That's what working in an organization is all about. There is no reason in the world, on the other hand, for your taking a beating from BE. To do so is to invite unneeded stress and misery into your life. That nobody needs or deserves.

13
What If?

My experience tells me that when DPs are confronted according to my principles, change is likely to result. In fact, stand by to be amazed. Why such dramatic results? It's elementary. You have stripped DP bare. He has nowhere to hide. To pursue their former cause would suggest they really are emotionally ill. Their only intelligent option is to re-enter the human race. Can I guarantee that? No! But I'll give some odds: 90% of the time, or more, expect much better behavior. How about the 10% who don't change? As with all DPs, you must persist. And you may wish to modify your approach. Here are the most common what-ifs and the best ways to operate. What if:

1. *There's no change?* What follows is standard advice for use when any DP refuses to change. First, persist (Remember that?). You've got to be as stubborn as they are. They're trying to wear you down. You must do the same. That means keeping the pressure on until something happens. Unless they are totally oblivious to how people are reacting to them, they'll begin to change. From their point of view, you are beginning to drive them crazy. And they don't like your treatment any more than you like theirs. So unless they want to walk around with barrels of mental distress, they're going to have to sue for peace.

Secondly, take a good look at your methods. Maybe you need a new approach. Add something new. But don't change until you're sure he's gotten the original message. DPs have a tendency not to hear the first time around. I'd confront a DP essentially the same way over a few weeks before I abandoned that basic approach. After that—sure, you may need a change of tactic. Remember, however, that my approach has been tested. It has been found to work better than any competing approach. Be slow to abandon it.

2. *It turns out to be a hopeless case?* If I could guarantee that every DP would change for the better by your applying my formula, it would be magic. We all know that's impossible. In life we play the odds. We go with the most rational plan available to us. That's what I've given you. When it becomes clear that the cause is a lost one, we exercise our options. Here's my advice: Before negotiating with DP, consider what will happen if you fail—that is, she doesn't shape up. What options do you have? Here's a rundown on a few popular ones that people tell me they have successfully employed.

- *Enlist others.* It's called group pressure. It's potent. Now DP has more than one person on his back. You get relevant others to join you. Does it work? Very often. The reason it works is that DP may have shrugged you off as being "just one" unhappy individual. When the numbers grow it gets harder and harder to rationalize. The pressure mounts. Better behavior follows.
- *Confront DP in the presence of a significant other.* Significant others are the very important people in our lives: the boss, our spouse, our pastor, valued colleagues, or very close friends. This is not a simple case of enlisting others. It's a case of enlisting a very special

other in DP's life. Assumption: DP doesn't want to look stupid and insensitive to a significant other. Hence there may be an immediate cessation of hostilities. One thing: Don't bring in one of DP's significant others without ample warning. The very fact that you threaten to do so may impact on her. Hopefully the result will be better treatment of you. This is another way of saying: Keep your flag unfurled!

- *Be prepared to cut off————*. DP is informed that her continued maltreatment of you will lead directly to your cutting off————from this moment on. And what possibly can we effectively cut off (or withhold)?
    - Affection.
    - Support.
    - Cooperation.
    - Money.
    - Good Will.
    - Services (of all kinds).
    - Favors (of all kinds).
    - Communication (Known as the silent treatment).

The list is hardly exhaustive. In short, find out what will hurt the most. Then proceed with the withholding. If DP doesn't yield under these pressures, then he can no longer be classified as a DP. "Oblivious" would be a more apt word.

- *Increase your capacity for living with it.* This, too, is a fundamental tenet in dealing with DPs. If you can't change DP, nothing works, and you can't leave—you're left with two alternatives. First, you may have to live with DP's behavior without letting it unduly upset you. But it doesn't stop there. You persist, no matter what. You never give in. You never give up trying to change DP. If it takes a lifetime, then it takes a lifetime.

14
DPs: Am I Becoming One?

In the earlier part of my research on DPs I asked this question: "Do you realize that some people in this organization have you labeled a DP?" The answer was always Yes. I assumed, therefore, that all DPs were well aware of their image. I was wrong.

It didn't take long for me to figure out that some people had no idea that others considered them DPs. I'd put the number at about 5% of the population. These are the people who often think that they are very much loved by everyone in the organization. In fact, nobody may love them, or even like them!

When I tell people of this statistic they naturally bring up the question "How do I know if others consider me a DP?" My initial response is that because we have our blind spots, we may not know.

The best way to find out is to ask periodically. If you push people hard enough they'll level with you. Their first reaction may well be one of embarrassment, or they may say that they think you are OK. That's what you've got to get beyond.

Are there any other ways of knowing? Lots of them. Here is what my sample told me were the most telling signs:

Avoidance. There is a drop off in people engaging you in conversation, for any reason. Some see you less frequently; others not at all.

Brief conversations. Except for the minimum courtesies, people are all business. They rarely linger.

They avoid being alone with you. You are the first to arrive for a meeting. You sit down. Someone else comes through the door. They see you sitting there. Suddenly, they have to go back to their office, or to the rest room. To be alone with you would be too anxiety-producing. They don't see you as being fun to talk to, or it may be their way of punishing you.

Social, small talk is out. The light conversation, the jokes—these have all but disappeared.

They seem unrelaxed. On the nonverbal level, they seem stiff. The smiles are not there. Posture is rigid. They seem not to enjoy being there.

The atmosphere has changed. You feel you can cut it with a knife. There is a lack of good feeling, of liking for one another. When you compare it with other times, you conclude that relationships have deteriorated.

There is an increase in soft talk. By soft talk I mean talk you can barely hear unless you are right next to the person. People aren't talking up any more.

A change in verbal interaction. In small group meetings—formal or informal—people aren't sending their conversation in your direction. This means they are not asking your opinion or approval of an idea. You feel like there are two groups: you versus the rest of the world.

A generalized feeling of isolation. Across the board you feel like you are not in the mainstream of communication within the organization. You feel there is an organized plot to keep you sequestered.

Eyeballs roll when you talk. You talk and the other people present roll their eyes and glance at each other as if to say: "There he goes again." or "Can you believe this woman?"

Rewarding behavior diminishes. Fewer and fewer compliments come your way. The little things we all do for each other—like getting coffee—drop to zero.

Now What?

Depending on how long people have perceived you as a DP you may have received nothing directly. You're still wondering. If I can assume for the moment you have become a DP without becoming aware of it, then there is hope. Advice:

Massive feedback. Get it! Don't delay. Do it now. Grab everyone in sight. Ask them the same question. "How do you see me?" "Am I going astray? If so, how and where?"

You'll be embarrassed. So will they. That's your problem—and theirs. You need the information. So put your ego on hold. When you've gone through it, you'll feel great. For the first time in your life you will probably have communicated very well indeed.

Evaluating the feedback. It's one thing to get feedback. It's quite another to sort it out for meaning. For one thing, you may have mutually contradictory messages from different people. Which one is the right one? You don't know. For another, people may suggest that you should be saying Yes more of the time. Upon analysis, you find out that you are doing things according to the organization's rules. You can't say Yes unless the rules say you can.

In short, feedback is often confusing and hard to understand. There's a message there, but you aren't entirely sure what it is.

Don't change abruptly. You could be getting yourself in deeper than you already are. The word is "ponder." Reflect on where each of their suggestions might lead you both in the short and long runs. Then decide what changes you are going to make.

There are some changes you can and should make immediately. For example, if you are accused of engaging in inhumane behavior, of treating others like dirt, you have no options. You must stop it. It isn't debatable and no sorting out is required.

Getting feedback on your new behavior. Once you are on the road to doing things differently you will want to know if your image is changing. It probably is. Just don't take it for granted.

Ask for new feedback whenever you do something that you think represents an improvement in your behavior. This serves to let people know that you are committed to change. And it sensitizes them to specific steps you are taking.

Stay in touch. If there is a great principle of communication it's this: the people we talk to regularly tend to stick by us. It's that part of communication that is a great medicine. Not a cure necessarily, but great medicine. It suggests that the people who become alienated from us because of our behavior are often those we ignore or talk to infrequently. Put another way, we can't get feedback from people we aren't talking to.

15
Your Fighting Back Profile

Over six thousand people have responded to this fighting back profile. I invite you to check your profile against theirs. Simply encircle the *one* response that best describes how you see yourself. Send it, along with a self-addressed stamped envelope, to Dr. Raymond K. Tucker, P.O. Box 132, Bowling Green, Ohio 43402. I'll show you where you stand with respect to the other six thousand.

The Scale: A = Agree Definitely
a = agree Somewhat
? = Undecided, or Neutral
d = disagree Somewhat
D = Disagree Definitely

1. I fear no one.	A	a	?	d	D
2. I am easily intimidated.	A	a	?	d	D
3. I often don't know what to say.	A	a	?	d	D
4. I avoid talking to people who seem to have power.	A	a	?	d	D
5. Loud people scare me.	A	a	?	d	D
6. I feel I can stand up to anyone.	A	a	?	d	D
7. Confronting someone face to face is easy for me.	A	a	?	d	D
8. I think of myself as a communicatively powerful person.	A	a	?	d	D
9. I tend to think the other person's communicative skills are better than mine.	A	a	?	d	D
10. If I feel I am right I will not give in.	A	a	?	d	D
11. My solution to difficult people is to avoid them.	A	a	?	d	D
12. I am not easily bluffed.	A	a	?	d	D

16
Contact Information

Dr. Raymond K. Tucker
Chair, Department of Interpersonal and Public Communication
Bowling Green State University
Bowling Green, Ohio 43403
Telephone: 419–372–7168

OR

941 MELROSE STREET
BOWLING GREEN, OHIO 43402
Telephone: 419–352–0511

OR

R. K. Tucker, Inc.
BOX 132
BOWLING GREEN, OHIO 43402